The Secrets of Managing a Successful Childcare Center

Real World Experience

with Lessons From the Field

Andrea Hendon Busch, Ed.D.

Dedication

This book is dedicated to my three wonderful children Cameron, Taryn, and Kristyn who bring great joy to my life. Experiencing early childhood through each of them created my own understanding of the immense importance of high quality early childhood programs. I realized how those programs can really make a difference in children's lives both during early childhood and throughout life.

The Secrets of Managing a Successful Childcare Center

Real World Experience with Lessons From the Field

Copyright © 2013 Andrea Hendon Busch, Ed.D.
All rights reserved.

All rights reserved. No part of this book may be generated or transmitted in any form or by any means, electronic or mechanical, including photocopying, recording, or by any information storage or retrieval system, without the permission of the publisher.

Published by
Building Blocks Books
P.O. Box 623, Liverpool, TX 77577

Acknowledgements

I am grateful to Janella Hendon, Betsy White, and Delaine Day who were my editors. I greatly appreciate the hours they each spent reading and providing input into the quality of this book. I want to thank my husband Todd, for his endless support and understanding of my projects. I also appreciate the opportunity to work with many children and families over the years. I've enjoyed the opportunities to develop programs for children and watch them learn and grow within those programs. I am grateful to all of the parents who entrusted me with their children's safety, well being, and early childhood education.

Notice to the Reader

This book is designed to provide relevant information based on real experiences within the field of early childhood. It is not intended to be a comprehensive resource. It provides information based on the real experiences of the author and others through input and research. The information provided should be used within the readers own context, good judgment, and appropriate professional advice as needed. Despite the best efforts of both the author and publisher, the book may contain mistakes, either typographical or in content. The book should be used as a guide along with other professional information and should not be used as the ultimate source of information on the subject. The reader is solely responsible for actions taken within his or her own early childhood program. This relates to all subject matter including both theory and practice. This book is sold without warranties of any kind and the publisher and author are not responsible for any liability, loss, or damages from the reader's use of the book and its content.

Contents

Preface 1

Introduction 3

Chapter 1: Managing with Heart 5

Chapter 2: Local Regulations 11

Chapter 3: State Childcare Regulations and Records 17

Chapter 4: State Inspections and Investigations 23

Chapter 5: Children's Safety 37

Chapter 6: Children's Health 55

Chapter 7: Supervision of Young Children 67

Chapter 8: Outdoor Supervision 73

Chapter 9: School-Age Programs 79

Chapter 10: Food Service 87

Chapter 11: Staffing: Hiring, Releasing, and Retaining 99

Chapter 12: Staff Training 115

Chapter 13: Staff Supervision 123

Chapter 14: Staff Health and Safety 133

Chapter 15: Teachers and Their Own Children 137

Chapter 16: Children's Behaviors 141

Chapter 17: Parents' Behaviors 151

Chapter 18: Financial Management 159

Chapter 19: Records Management 167

Chapter 20: Facilities Management 173

Chapter 21: Curriculum and Environment 181

Chapter 22: Sustaining Long Term Success 187

Preface

Walking into an attractive and well managed childcare center is a wonderful experience! Clean colorful rooms are filled with child size furnishings, materials, toys, art supplies and most of all happy busy children. It's an almost perfect world where children with smiling faces play together and learn in a positive and productive environment. It's what childcare center owners, directors, teachers, and parents all desire for their children. When it is done well, it provides benefits for children that will last a lifetime.

I vividly remember how good it felt to have my first child in a wonderful early childhood center. I felt good about the teachers taking care of him, the level of care, his early childhood education, and his preschool social life. Some days, when I arrived in the afternoon, my enthusiastic three year old would ask me to pick him up later … after all of the other children had gone home! Later when I owned my own center, I truly enjoyed those moments when children at my center would ask their parents essentially the same thing … and yes, sometimes parents would leave and come back closer to closing time, so their children could continue to enjoy all the activities.

The dream of owning a childcare center or directing a center must come from the heart. It's much more than a business and extends much further than the bottom line found on a financial statement. It encompasses a true love for children and a desire to make a difference in their lives.

What appears to be an easy job: watching children play, reading books to them, and creating projects is actually a very complex and multifaceted world. There are a number of books available which address how to start a childcare center and there are resources for financial management of centers. In contrast, there is little information available on the realities of the ongoing management and long term sustainability of childcare centers. Establishing a licensed center is a huge process and it is quite a statement of success to reach that point. However, that is just the beginning. Individuals enter the business after successfully accomplishing the establishment and licensing processes. Then they are often abruptly faced with some of the harsher realities of the childcare business. I've watched this occur numerous times. There isn't much available that prepares individuals for the more striking realities of the business.

Before opening a childcare center, I read many books. A few contained cryptic lists with concerning events that had happened in childcare centers. These included things such as: minor to severe injuries; burns; children being left on a field trip; and other concerns. As bad as these things sounded, I had no real concern. I knew that I wouldn't let those things happen ... the realities came later.

The realities from reading such simplistic lists didn't prepare me for the growth and staff management issues that occur. These difficulties occur when you are no longer able to be in all of the rooms and control every aspect of the center. At that point, you become dependent on others to provide the same care and safety in your absence. The larger the center, the harder it becomes to maintain that hands-on approach. In addition, the more people you employ, the harder it is to find those staff members who truly take the care that you would take in each and every step.

This is the "other" book that I wish I could have read prior to going into the childcare business. It addresses many of the realities of the complicated day to day "real world" of childcare. It is written to provide the knowledge and tools necessary to make childcare centers truly exceptional in the long run. This is accomplished through providing insight into ways to handle difficult situations and even preventing situations from occurring in the first place. It will make difficult situations less stressful as you (the owner, director, or manager) recognize that many of the most difficult situations are a part of the work. You are not alone in having to deal with such issues. Knowledge and experience provide the foundation for ongoing sustainable success.

Much can be learned from the experiences of others including real stories and reviewing state licensing reports. This book is based on my own years of experience along with talking to others in the field. It also includes volumes of research in public citations obtained over a ten year period. The information provides a comprehensive look into the real work, complexities, and challenges in the field of childcare. It will provide information that takes many owners years to gain through tough experiences.

Whether you are considering starting a childcare business; in the early stages of your business operation; or you are looking for real world solutions to your daily challenges; let me be your consultant. Just as if I were in your center and talking to you, as you read through the pages of the book, I will share with you years of experiences, practical insights, and solutions in the challenging field of childcare.

Introduction

Many people enter the field of childcare with preconceived ideas about what the work entails. Those ideas do not usually parallel with the realities of the business. The vision that you see as you enter a childcare center is very different from the one of someone who is working on the inside. High quality childcare centers appear to be sweet and happy places where teachers' and directors' days are filled with watching happy children play and painting pictures alongside them. Unfortunately, this is how easy many parents think the job is as well.

In reality, it is multi-faceted and complex. It includes balancing many areas including: safety; supervision of children; hiring and training of staff; ongoing supervision of staff; overseeing curriculum and teaching; extensive bookkeeping and regulatory paperwork; state inspections; local inspections; maintaining supplies; managing children's behaviors; dealing with parent concerns; marketing and continuing to show the school; maintaining facilities and equipment; food service; and much more. It is a complex business with many dimensions and the center of it all is the children. It is extremely challenging work but very meaningful. No other job is more important than one that offers the highest level of early childhood education, care, and safety of children.

Events that create concern happen even in the best of centers. I constantly studied licensing information and reviewed citations of centers as a means of staying on top of all of the safety and regulatory issues. This is public information in many states and accessible through the state childcare licensing. Knowledge gives you the power to prevent many issues and the skill to handle the ones that you can't prevent.

The terms manager, owner, and director are used interchangeably throughout the book to refer to the individual who is in charge at the center. Some of these positions are held by one individual and in other cases, the positions are held by more than one person. The terms teacher, caregiver, employee, and staff member are also used interchangeably to refer to those employed by the center who work with children. The term parent refers to the primary custodial person. It can encompass parents, grandparents, foster parents, guardians and others who have the full legal responsibility for children in the center. References to gender, such as he or she, are used interchangeably throughout the book. In addition, all names have been changed when referring to real world examples and childcare centers as the information is provided for educational purposes and not to identify any person or center. Each chapter covers a particular area. Some details may overlap in an attempt to create a more comprehensive understanding of pertinent information in each chapter.

I operated a licensed childcare center in the state of Texas and there are referrals to regulations of that state. Each state has its own regulatory agency and regulations developed and enforced by that agency. Refer to your own state regulations, for full information on the specific requirements that apply to your center.

No part of the book is considered to be legal advice. All actions within every childcare business should be completed with the highest of moral and legal standards. Training seminars often include legal information and even lawyers who work in the field of childcare. It is beneficial for those in the industry to study legal issues surrounding the business of childcare. Even so, there are times when it is necessary to seek the legal advice of an attorney who specializes in the childcare industry.

Done well, owning or directing a high quality childcare center is very rewarding. An excellent early childhood education center provides young children with the foundation for a lifetime of success. The benefits of a quality early childhood program are well researched and documented. This is an important industry where the business and financial elements must always be balanced with program benefits for the children. This is a business that takes heart.

1

Managing with Heart

In this chapter, you will discover the basic concepts for managing a successful early childhood center including:

- Setting the Stage
- The Role of Directors/Owners
- Managing the Daily Complexities

Setting the Stage

Creating a wonderful and welcoming environment for children is a vital component of a quality childcare center. Children and parents should feel welcome every morning. They should be greeted by happy early childhood teachers who truly love the children. It should "feel" good. This sets the stage for the entire day and for the overall center environment. When they have concerns, parents should be reassured that their children will have a great day.

The often short moments of drop off time, are absolutely crucial. Make sure the stage is set for a great day for children. Also, be there for the parents, as they trust you with the care of their precious children. Make sure they are confident and feel good about their child's day. Your staff is the key to creating this atmosphere. There are always going to be days when staff members don't want to be at work because they don't feel well, lack of sleep, outside stresses, and a host of other possible reasons. Simply reinforce that part of the job is to appear happy and positive for both children and parents. There is no more important time for this than at drop off.

❖ Lesson From the Field: Positive Greetings

I included the requirements for greeting every child by name in the training program. It was expected and required that mornings were a happy time. Teach your staff that if they don't feel it, they must "fake it" but the atmosphere must be positive and happy. This is part of the job.

Positive drop off extends to parents as well. Their attitude and behaviors while dropping off their children can have a huge impact on how the children react.

❖ Lesson From the Field: Drop Off Procedures

I always advised the parents at my center that drop offs should be "fast and happy." When parents wanted to stay and join us, it worked best at the end of the day. Parents should feel good about their children's daily activities and should always feel welcome to be a part of the school; however, lingering too long at drop off can set a different stage. Children can become upset and want to go with their parents. The assurance that it's going to be a great day, works for parents too. They can feel the energy and enthusiasm.

One of the hardest ways to start a day is when the parent feels guilty and apologetic for bringing the child to the center. The parent stays longer. The child often cries because the delay gives her time to think longer about being dropped off and the possibility that the parent might take her back home for the day. Fast and happy drop offs also manage to keep that morning line of cars in the driveway moving, which can be very important when other parents are trying to get to work.

As the director, you should make it a point to be there at least some of the times when parents are dropping off their children and picking them up as well. This provides parents the opportunity to communicate with you about important details or just chat about how happy they are with what their child has learned. It allows for parents to be connected to the management of the childcare center, not just their child's teacher. It also allows for the director to be more aware of what is going on simply by being in the middle of things. This provides those informal opportunities to speak with parents. These connections are really important when the big issues come up … and there will be some. Parents, who feel connected to the center's management, will bring you small issues just to let you know. When issues are fixed that way, very few of them will turn into big problems. The ones that do turn into problems will be easier to resolve due to the personal connection with the center's management.

It's also important to note that happy and connected parents are your best source of marketing. Word of mouth advertising is free and more productive than almost any other advertising you will do. A great program with happy parents creates its own marketing.

❖ Lesson From the Field: Word of Mouth Marketing

After the earliest months in the business, our best advertisement came from parent referrals. The parents were very happy with what their children were learning. They were amazed that their children appeared to be much more advanced than other children their age in academics, discipline, and abilities. They readily shared the information with their friends, who would then seek us out and were sold on our programs before they ever set foot inside the building.

The Role of Directors/Owners

Childcare should be a "hands-on" business. The quality is highly correlated to the on-site management. Having someone in charge, who is there every day, is an integral part of the daily operations. In the best situations, a quality childcare center should be managed by someone who is there on a daily basis to oversee all of the details and carefully supervise both the staff and the children's programs. This person provides the support and foundation for all the activities both from the business management perspective and from the childcare perspective.

The role of the owner, or director, is very complex as it is multi-faceted. There is always a balance between the business needs and the children's needs. For example, the best ratio for children would be the lowest ratio of children to staff possible. A one to one ratio is fantastic for a child but it obviously doesn't correspond to a business model. On the opposite extreme, having as many children per adult as possible correlates well from a business standpoint but doesn't make a quality program and doesn't benefit children. The childcare licensing division for your state will dictate the maximum number of children per adult which is allowed. (States vary in their regulations including ratio requirements.) Just because the state allows a particular number of children does not mean that is the appropriate number to be assigned to one staff member. The program, teacher, and the individual children in the classroom can all impact what is an appropriate ratio for the room.

Managing a program with your heart, means always keeping in mind what is best for the children and still being able to manage the business end of the childcare center. Establish a quality center with excellent programs that comply with all of your state standards. Then create a tuition rate which will allow the business to be viable and you have created your balance. There is a market for high quality programs and many parents will pay more tuition for a really good children's program. Do not try to compete by being the cheapest. It's a bad business model and it doesn't allow the funds needed for a high quality program. Managing a high quality program does lead to higher business expenses. Be open and explain why it is worth a higher tuition rate for your program. The right balance allows for a sustainable and successful childcare center which provides high quality programs. There is much more discussion on the balance of quality programs and finances in later chapters.

Managing the Daily Complexities

As the manager of a childcare center, you really never know what the day will bring. Surprises such as children's accidents and injuries, staff absences and emergencies, allergic reactions, illnesses, and upset parents can all occur in an instant. Some days will run smoothly and the managerial paperwork and supervision will flow as planned. Other days, it's as if nothing on the planned "to do list" will get done because the entire day is filled with those surprises. As always, the children and their needs will come first.

Your days will often begin very early and end very late. The hours of operation do not dictate the work hours of a good childcare manager. You will have staff calling late at night or early in the morning to let you know they are ill and can't be at work. Emergencies occur at all hours which impact your day's operation. It is important to be available to your staff at all hours. It's much better to get a call that someone will be out the next day at 11:00 PM than it is to get that same call 30 minutes before you open. A late night call gives you time to make phone calls; try to get another staff member to cover the position; or let someone know she will need to work extra hours the next day. The earlier the notice, the sooner you are able to get the schedule adjusted for the next day.

Handling issues after hours for parents is also common. Even though you may choose not to give your personal number out to all parents, you will still find yourself handling situations with parents after hours. An example of this is when a child is injured and has to go to the doctor. It is a good idea to make that phone call and connect with the parent after everything is better. It lets you know how serious the injury was; provides information you need to document; and lets the parent know that you really care about her child.

If you believe a parent will be angry, it is best to stay at the center until the parent arrives so that you can handle it in person; however, you do not always know when this is going to happen. Calling parents in the evening is necessary. If a parent is angry, for some reason, when they pick up a child and you were not there; the staff on duty should notify you and provide you with the parent's number from the center's files. Again, calling at night shows you care and can help to resolve issues. It can also help you sleep better because you don't have to worry all night about what faces you in the morning.

❖ Lesson From the Field: Pebble in Mitchell's Ear

Mitchell was once again lying in the pebbles on the playground after being required to get up twice before. His friend, Jerry tossed some pebbles at him and then Mitchell said that one of them was stuck in his ear. There wasn't a pebble visible and it didn't appear that one was in his ear. However, he insisted, and erring on the conservative side, I reported that we needed to call his mother. The other teachers on duty quickly looked at me and said they didn't want to have to report the incident to "this mother." She had a tendency to react dramatically. I called and explained the situation to the parent. She appeared to be fine with the situation and said she would come to the center and check on Mitchell. I left my cell phone number for her so that she could call me later that evening.

Even though I had called, and tried to make sure that the parent was not upset before I left for the day, when she arrived at the center it did not go smoothly for the staff on duty. She directed her anger toward the teachers. She wanted to know how this could happen. She stated that there must not have been enough teachers on duty and said they should have been able to prevent this incident. She accused the teachers of allowing other children to throw rocks at her child; she even suggested that other children had intentionally pushed the pebble into his ear. Mitchell's mother didn't call me that evening so I went ahead and called her. There indeed had been a rock inside his ear and it had to be removed by the doctor. We talked and worked things out. I always preferred when possible to smooth things out so we could all sleep better and not worry about what the next day would bring.

Situations, such as this example, make the already complex job of caregivers even more difficult. When at all possible, I tried to alleviate this by being the one to handle the very difficult situations. Still, as in this case, the brunt of an angry parent can fall onto teachers at times.

Taking care of all of the children's issues first will mean that on many weekends, you will find yourself going back to the center to complete all of the paperwork that is still sitting on your desk. Unless you outsource all of your facilities maintenance duties, you will often find yourself completing those on the weekends as well. Maintenance and heavy cleaning duties in particular, usually need to be completed after hours and on weekends as these may include activities which would create safety hazards for children. In addition, purchasing and stocking food and supplies (if you don't have these delivered) will often be done after operational hours.

Even with all of the love for children, quality programs and staff, and dedication to care that you put into your business, you will still here inappropriate referrals to yourself and your program. One of the most offensive statements you will hear is: "She is just in it for the money." They don't know the realities! There are many easier ways to make money including industries with much higher profit margins. Money alone, isn't a reason that anyone should go into the field; however, it's almost guaranteed you will hear this statement and probably more than once. Statements like this come from unhappy staff members, parents, and others who lack the understanding of how much "heart" goes into your business. It makes you want to provide long responses of how much you dedicate to the center. However, it's a statement that you should just ignore and continue on with your convictions of providing the absolute best for the children in your care.

2

Local Regulations

In this chapter, you will discover how local codes and insurance impact your business including:

- Local Permits and Inspections
- Staying Current with Changing Codes
- Fire Alarms
- Insurance Requirements and Restrictions
- Other Applicable Regulations
- Connections Between Licensing and Local Codes

Local Permits and Inspections

Local regulations are required to open your childcare business; you are also required to keep them up to date. The best way to do this is to keep a calendar of when each of the local inspections and regulations must be updated. These details generally fall under the state regulations as well. Your state inspector will likely be checking to make sure that you are in full compliance with the local requirements. Regulations in Texas (and other states) require full compliance with local codes and state inspectors require you to provide this documentation to them.

These local regulations, which are required by your local governing agency (usually the city in which you operate), will most likely include: an annual renewal of your permit to operate in the city or county; an annual health inspection; renewing your food service permit if you are managing a commercial kitchen; documentation of monthly fire drills; gas pipe testing if you have gas connections to the building; and a fire inspection. The fire inspection is often multi-faceted. In order to pass a fire inspection, it is often necessary that all of your fire extinguishers have been inspected, dated, and re-charged if necessary; your alarm system has been inspected by the alarm company; and then the fire marshal or other representative completes a full inspection. In order to pass the inspection, the fire inspector will most likely require the other updates to have already been completed and documented.

Be aware that fire inspections, both inspections of the system and the final inspection by the local fire department, may include setting off your fire alarms. In a building filled with small children, this is not fun at any time; it's even worse if it comes at lunch or nap time. If at all possible, schedule such inspections. If you are allowed to schedule them, make sure it is set for a time when it will be the least disruptive to your children and program.

Another helpful suggestion is to make sure that, if the children are going to need to evacuate the building, you time the evacuation and count it as a fire drill. It makes good sense to utilize it and you have one more thing completed. If it has to be done, document it.

Most local permits will expire and need to be renewed annually. These should be on your schedule at least a few weeks before they are due to expire. This allows time to request the inspection and get onto the inspector's schedule so that the inspection is completed before the permit expires. Some local inspections may be unannounced and on the local inspector's agenda; however, many of these are done based on a request. In the latter case, if you don't request the local inspections, yours will expire. This will then lead to a state licensing violation when your inspector arrives and the permits are out of date.

Staying Current with Changing Codes

Local codes and requirements can change at any time. Usually these changes will come with written notice in advance, allowing you time to comply with code changes. Just as with state licensing updates, usually these changes cost you money, and sometimes significant amounts. Local codes vary and so the updates will likewise vary from city to city as well as state to state.

The most dramatic examples of change that I experienced over the years in my own childcare center were local fire codes. These ranged from simple to complex and expensive.

❖ Lesson From the Field: Moderate Fire Code Change

An example of a simple change was the requirement that battery backup lighting had to be permanently attached and wired into the building. Prior to this requirement, having a battery operated flashlight available in each room was sufficient to meet both state and local standards for battery back-up lighting. With this change, the local standards became stricter than the state standards. This was not an expensive update. It required going to a local home improvement store; purchasing battery back-up lights that could be permanently installed; and permanently attaching these to the wall. The new lighting units plugged into an outlet which kept them charged.

❖ Lesson From the Field: Significant Fire Code Change

A much more extensive and very expensive change was another fire code change a few years later. This update stated that in order to continue to operate a full commercial kitchen (to continue to use the stove top and oven), we were required to have a large commercial piece of equipment installed over the stove top. This equipment contained a chemical that would spray down on the stove in the case of a fire. It also included the addition of an extremely large and heavy fire extinguisher mounted inside the kitchen, in case of grease fires (even though we never fried food). All of the new equipment had to be purchased and installed. After installation, it had to be connected into the existing fire alarm and monitoring system by the company that managed our fire alarm system.

Many centers at that time could not afford the thousands of dollars required to comply with the new code. Those centers began using microwaves or other methods to adjust their food service processes to a point where they didn't have to purchase the equipment. We met the new codes and then we let all of our parents know; we would continue to operate a full commercial kitchen and provide the quality meals that they wanted for their children. As always, I did what I believed was best for the children in my center and then I made sure that I let the parents and others know all of the good things that we provided.

Expenses like this are a huge issue. The thousands of dollars that went into the purchase, installation, and tying the equipment into the existing fire system would have been income. There is a higher cost to running a childcare center with a focus on providing well for children, while diligently meeting all of the increasing regulatory requirements.

Fire Alarms

Our local fire codes, as with many centers, required 24 hour a day monitoring which included an automatic call to the fire department if the alarms were set off. It is good as a protective measure, but it also means you have no control over the process. If the alarms go off ... expect the fire department!

❖ Lesson From the Field: The Burning Hot Dog

The only "fire" we ever had in the building was that of a hot dog wiener that was dropped on the stove top. It caught on fire and smoked up the kitchen. This set off the alarms and required a building evacuation. The fire system procedures went into effect and automatically called out the fire department.

Not only did it disrupt the schedule, screaming fire trucks arrived at the center, and nervous parents called as they heard reports of a fire. The building was inspected before the children and staff were allowed to return inside. A note was sent home with each child explaining the situation (as you will read often throughout the book – good communication with parents is absolutely essential).

This particular incident happened in our early years and the results were dramatic enough. If it had happened after the installation of the overhead system, it would have been even more dramatic! The simple error of the cook dropping a wiener on the stove top would have resulted in the full expelling of foam all over the stove top area in the kitchen; a major clean up; along with the complete re-setting of the system so that the system would continue to pass inspection. The protection by automatic notification of the fire department is good in its intent, but sometimes it feels excessive when a simple act sets off a huge chain of events.

Insurance Requirements and Restrictions

Another area that is really important for your center, which can change is insurance. State regulations usually require you to maintain a specified value of insurance liability. Unlike local and state regulations, which will be the same for everyone in the area, the insurance policy that you have may vary greatly from a center just down the road. Take the time to talk to your insurance representative and understand what your policy covers and any restrictions it contains. This should be done annually when you renew your insurance policy.

❖ Lesson From the Field: Insurance Restrictions

The insurance policy that we utilized put restrictions on such things as swimming. We were allowed to have splash days with wading pools, but swimming was not covered. This is important to note because a number of other childcare centers, in our town, either took their children swimming or even had a pool on site. This regulation had little real impact on my center as I didn't want to include swimming in our programs. Even with appropriate number of teachers supervising, a group of swimming children is a big safety concern. Other insurance regulations and changes did impact what I could include in the children's program.

I watched as insurance regulations became stricter over time. It was necessary to remove the inflatable water slide that I purchased for the center. The children enjoyed this fun summer activity for a couple of years; then the regulations changed, and water slides were not allowed or covered by our insurance company any more. These changes are often the result of law suits brought over time. Expect policies to change based on current trends of activities, injuries, and law suits that the insurance companies have to defend.

Other Applicable Regulations

You may also fall under county and state regulations outside of childcare regulations. These can include disclosing "reportable" illnesses to your health department. It can also include audits of your health records; filing reports such as hearing and vision screenings; and filing forms on how many children are fully vaccinated. At one time, I was even contacted by an FBI agent that a missing child was seen at my center.

❖ Lesson From the Field: FBI Investigation

A young elementary age child, who had only been with us for a short time was with her father at a local store when she saw the posters of missing children. She told him that she had seen one of those children at the center. He called the number listed on the poster which then set out an investigation to find out if the child had been seen at my center. I took one look at the picture and said the child had not been there. I knew all of the children and families well and had no doubt that the information was wrong. This went on for awhile as I provided all of the requested information so that they could rule out this lead as legitimate.

Connections between Licensing and Local Codes

State childcare licensing will typically require you to be up to date on all local codes. Refer to the childcare regulations for your state for the specific details. The Texas childcare regulations require you to be in full compliance with all of these local standards or you will have a violation from the state along with other issues which may arise from a lack of compliance with the local inspectors. If there is a deficiency in a local code inspection, it should be immediately corrected and a re-inspection scheduled. The re-inspection and correction will bring your local requirements into compliance prior to having a state inspector review them.

❖ Lesson From the Field: Conflicting Regulations

One year, a parent didn't want her child to be required to have a hearing and vision screening, which was part of routine state health requirements along with vaccinations. The parent proceeded to go to the health department to get a waiver so that her child was not required to have the screening. Without prior knowledge that the parent had done this, I received a notice that stated this particular child did not have to have a hearing and vision screening based on the fact that he attended only two days per week. The health department representative classified this child as attending a mother's day out program. This was in direct contradiction to our state childcare regulations.

I sent an email to the writer of the letter, and stated "Please provide a policy statement that is applicable to all children. This is important unless you are making an exception for only one child. I need to know in order to appropriately take care of the records required by your office. In addition, I will provide such notification to our licensing authority because we are not a mother's day out program and our regulations are based on the state licensing agency for childcare."

The return correspondence that I received stated:

"Dr. Busch,

Please be advised that I do not make exceptions for only one child. Our program policy is children who attend a center for less than three days a week are not required to have vision and hearing screens. Please do provide this information to your licensing authority and if they have any questions or concerns, inform them to contact me."

I kept the email and did provide it to my state licensing representative as no such leeway was provided in the childcare standards. She had never heard of such an exception and took her copy of the letter back to her supervisor. The rules didn't change and I never heard back from the inspector as to what her supervisor said regarding this exception to their rules.

We were a licensed childcare center, not a mother's day out where most programs were unregulated. The fact that some children only attended two days per week did not mean that we were then a mother's day out program for those children. We were still a licensed childcare center with all of the regulations of such. Our state regulations did not vary based on the number of days a child attended. I retained the documentation, both in the child's file and in our file of state licensing documents. This would be needed to cover any attempt by an inspector to cite this as a violation in the future. My own question remained. "If the health department thought it was very important for children at the age of four to be checked for early problems with vision and hearing; is it only important for children in licensed programs?"

3

State Childcare Regulations and Records

In this chapter, you will discover the details of managing complicated state regulations and maintaining accurate auditable state required records including:

- Overview of Regulations and Records
- Changing Regulations
- Personnel Records - Background Checks and Fingerprinting
- State Required Recordkeeping

Overview of Regulations and Records

State licensing requirements and ongoing childcare center regulations vary by state. If you don't already have a copy, you should contact your state's childcare licensing entity and obtain a copy of the latest childcare standards for your center. (Most states will have this information online so that the regulations can be downloaded.) Childcare is a highly regulated business. For the childcare manager, this means that you will have many requirements to meet which will include areas from office files, public display postings, equipments requirements, and of course how the children's program is managed.

Childcare is highly regulated for a reason. The safety and quality of care for children is one of the most important concerns. All of the "rules" were written for a reason. The reasons encompass protecting children as well as protecting the center and staff (a reason for the large amount of documentation required). Remember the rules were written for specific reasons when you read your state's requirements for your center. Take note of some of the more unusual specifications. These are the ones where you ask yourself: "Did they have to make that a rule?" "Would someone really do that?" It's almost unbelievable some of the things that must be written down as rules. My favorite example of a rule is one in reference to serving food:

❖ Lesson From the Field: Food Service Regulations

"You must serve children's food on plates, napkins, or other sanitary holders such as a high chair tray and you must not place food on a bare table or eating surface, which includes the floor;"

Minimum Standards for Childcare Centers, Texas Department of Family and Protective Services, 2010, pg 105.

Is it necessary to specify that the centers are not to serve food off of the bare floor? The concerning part is that someone probably did that, for the agency to determine that it needs to be included in the rules.

Changing Regulations

After meeting all of the requirements and obtaining a license, you are far from set with state regulations. These can be updated at any time. New centers are required to meet the newest standards in order to obtain a license; however, once you have received the license, the changes may come with different implementation time frames.

Some regulations may go into effect on a particular day. Other regulations may allow your center to continue to operate and be "grandfathered in" and therefore, the changes are not required. Still other changes may allow you an extension of time in which to comply. The reality is that often those changing regulations affect the cost of running a quality center. When that happens, it is necessary to do more than just comply with the changes. It is important to assess the cost of those changes and how those costs will be incorporated. Your options include: just accepting the costs; attempt to enroll more students; increasing tuition to cover those additional expenses; or a combination of these.

During my years in childcare, I found that the Texas state regulations were updated often and sometimes quite dramatically. Regulatory changes continually happened, requiring the center's management to constantly update policies, procedures, and facilities as determined by those changes. One year the proposed changes were so dramatic and time consuming to complete, that we had to go ahead with preparations for those changes well in advance of the final approval by the state. In the end, much of the expense, planning, and preparation we had put forth weren't necessary; the most dramatic changes were not approved! The same proposed changes, although not approved, were very likely to come back at another point in time. Also be aware of changes and the forms provided by your state licensing agency which correspond to the changes. If you don't update your forms, you may find yourself with a violation such as this one:

❖ Lesson From the Field: Documenting Injuries

A child fell and cut her head. Her parents were called and she was taken to the emergency room. She received stitches and was fine. This injury, according to our state regulations required a "self-report" where you call and report the incident to the state. I did this, which led to an automatic investigation.

The investigator arrived, questioned those who were on duty at the time, assessed the situation, and determined that we were not at fault and there were no standard violations related to the incident ... except one. When the event occurred, I was new to the business, and I had used an incident form that had been replaced. My form did not have a place for the parent's signature so it was not signed. We received a violation for not having the form signed by the parent.

Regularly review any licensing changes and new forms which are created by your state regulatory agency. These generally can be accessed through your state licensing website. Look for new forms and replace your old ones as necessary. Whenever possible, it is best to use the forms provided by the state, because these should include all the required details such as the place for a parent signature on an incident report (which wasn't a part of the old state form clearly used prior to requiring the signature).

Keep up to date on all regulations and changes, as well as the related documentation and forms. Adhere closely to the state requirements for your childcare center in order to insure that your center is well managed and to gain an excellent reputation with your state inspector. Remember, essentially you want the same thing. Both of you want a safe environment and high quality care for children. An additional benefit of having a good reputation with your state licensing inspector is usually fewer inspections. This is because the inspector is confident that you are running the center according to the state requirements.

Personnel Records - Background Checks and Fingerprinting

Background checks are a critical part of insuring the safety of children. These should always be completed and results obtained prior to letting new employees come into your center. There really isn't an excuse for centers who fail to get this paperwork done. Do not allow individuals in your center who have not cleared all relevant background checks. The addition of fingerprinting is now required in many states. This adds another layer to the safety procedures.

Background check results can be another licensing technical difficulty. Most run smoothly. The individual either has offenses on the record that prohibits her from working in childcare or she has a clean record. The difficulty comes when background checks come back with minor offenses on them (such as one bad check written over a decade ago). These minor offenses do not prohibit someone from working in childcare; however, the ones received on the Texas forms (during my tenure) did not provide a cleared background check for the file. We couldn't include the confidential information in a file that is accessible to others; yet we weren't provided with a document that proved the individual was cleared of offenses relating to the state regulations. How did I handle this? A separate file was put in a place in a secured area that was only known to the few individuals who were left in charge and even they did not know what was in the file. It was not to be accessed unless required by the state during an inspection or investigation.

State Required Recordkeeping

Recordkeeping requirements will vary by state. Recordkeeping required by the state can be quite cumbersome. There are a lot of requirements and many of the violations in centers are based on not having perfect recordkeeping. Create schedules, set up reminders, and diligently keep up with required paperwork. It is an important aspect of having a quality childcare center in the eyes of the state. Here we will focus on records subject to inspection. Chapter 19: Recordkeeping provides a more complex look at required records for all aspects of the business.

❖ Lesson From the Field: Paperwork Details

On one of my first inspections after my center opened its doors, I received one single violation. The citation stated that I had not written the notation "NA" on the special needs section of a child without special needs. Nothing on the state paperwork was allowed to be blank. Being blank indicated to the inspector that the form was not complete. Many parents will leave such questions blank when the questions aren't applicable to the child. It is necessary to have the parent go back and fill in all the blanks that do not apply with some form of answer such as "NA."

These required records that you need to maintain are subject to state inspection and then there are additional records that you need for your own business documentation which are not auditable by the state. It may be beneficial to have more than one set of records. These separate records are divided into business records and auditable state records. The information required by the state must be accessible to the state; however, the business and personnel records may include far more than is required by the state. These records can include things such as notes on children's behaviors, documentation of events, parent conference information, and even confidential notes (such as a copy of documentation you filled out for a child's doctor to have him tested for developmental concerns). There may be information that you need to keep but you do not want the state to audit either for business reasons or for confidentiality issues for the child.

A good way to accommodate this is to set up a file drawer that contains everything the state requires and then have a separate filing system for things that are not part of the required state documents. Personnel records are another area which deserves confidentiality. The state will require a personnel file on each staff member; however, the state inspector doesn't need to know how much each employee makes, that an employee's wages are garnished, or that you have put a staff member on probation. Not only are these items not required by most state regulations, sharing the information with someone who is unauthorized could make you liable for a breach of confidentiality.

Records which are evaluated at almost every inspection can be handled differently. A good way to organize these records is to create a file or a notebook which includes all of the documents which will usually be included in the inspection. These records include items such as the fire inspection, health inspection, gas pipe test, and other documentation that must be repeated on an annual or semi-annual basis. This is an easy way to keep everything in one place and update it once a year or as required by the regulations. When the inspector asks for the documents, you can just hand her the file or notebook. This means that you do not have to search for various documents. It also shows the inspector that you maintain your documents well and you are prepared.

- ❖ Lesson From the Field: Documentation ASAP

On one particular afternoon, I got a call from our licensing inspector; she needed the most recent fire inspection within an hour. It wasn't hard to see that she was under a deadline and the fact that she didn't have it on file was a reflection of her work and records. I faxed the inspection document to her on time. If I had not, I'm sure it would have resulted in a standards violation based on not having it available. My concern was: What if I had been out during that one hour? From that time forward, I made sure that each time I updated our local inspections, I immediately faxed her a copy of the documents. This prevented such "paperwork emergencies" from happening in the future.

Providing updated center inspection documents as they came due had advantages. The inspector knew that I kept current on all the paperwork. This continued to keep my center in good standing and therefore under less scrutiny. Many centers do not keep up with the required paperwork in an accurate and timely manner.

- ❖ Lesson From the Field: Records Audit during State Inspections

Some paperwork items were requested on every visit by our inspector including staff member files. She would request files on specific teachers and would look to see that everything that was required, was complete in the file. In addition, she would always ask for a certain number of student files. She would ask me to bring her, for example, seven children's files. I chose files that I knew were complete. Children's files are a great deal of work and must be updated as they have birthdays, need required vaccinations, are due for state required hearing and vision screenings, etc. The inspector had the right to choose any files she wanted, but if she was going to ask me to choose, I was going to make sure I chose files that were up to date. It is inherent that choosing the correct files actually means that you are on top of all of your paperwork. In order to select complete files, you have to know which ones are complete and which ones you are still working on updating.

The reality is it's hard to always have parents do what the state wants them to do in perfect timing that meets the states requirements. For example, some insurance companies will not pay for four year old vaccinations until the child has actually turned four. This means that if a parent doesn't take the child to the doctor until the next week, and that file is inspected before that date, you will have a violation. It is difficult to make the real world run in perfect schedule to the states requirements. I always paid careful attention to records, but they weren't always completed perfectly and on time. You can't make parents take their children to the doctor on your schedule. Your only option is remove them from your program, or gently remind them (sometimes repeatedly) that the state requires these things for their child to be enrolled in a licensed childcare center.

4

State Inspections and Investigations

In this chapter, you will discover how to successfully manage state inspections and investigations including:

- State Inspections Overview
- Interpreting Regulations
- Preparing for Inspections
- Researching Inspection Reports
- State Inspections: What It's Really Like
- Final Routine Inspection Report
- Receiving a Deficiency
- State Investigations: What It's Really Like

State Inspections Overview

Most often inspections are those "surprise" visits where a state inspector shows up unannounced to check on the center and look into whether it is operating according to the state requirements. Usually, the better a center's compliance with regulations, the fewer inspections will be required. Poorly operated centers are usually inspected much more often; however, all licensed centers are subject to inspection on a regular basis to verify compliance with state mandated procedures.

Staff members are often very nervous about inspections. Spend the time preparing them for inspections and constantly referring to regulations so that they know them backwards and forwards. Knowledge helps to prepare them for inspections and make for overall better compliance. I actually had a new teacher that panicked at the sight of the inspector and couldn't even remember how many children she had in the room. An experienced teacher passing through the room took over as if it was her classroom.

Interpreting Regulations

Although regulations are set out and intended to be very specific, there is often room for interpretation. It pays to know your inspector well and how she would interpret a particular regulation. If an inspector cites a violation that you believe is subject to interpretation, you should ask her to explain her reasoning to you. You should know all of the regulations; however, the "rule book is thick." If you find that you are being cited for something that you don't remember being in the regulations, don't hesitate to ask the inspector to show it to you. Always have your copy of the regulations available and ready. Pull out your copy and have her show you the regulation for which you were cited.

If you disagree with the assessment, you can write it on the form with your signature and there should be a way to file for a review of the particular citation. Do be willing to stand up for yourself if you believe your inspector is in error; however, choose to go forward only if you are sure and proceed with care. Making your state inspector into your adversary is not in your best interest.

Preparing for inspections

The most important part of being prepared for inspections is to manage your childcare center as if every day was a day that the state inspector is going to show up. A vital point is to make sure your staff knows what to do when you are visited by an inspector. Following all of the requirements, ratios, policies, and schedules which meet your licensing standards is good business and makes the center run the way that it should.

There are centers that operate outside of the regulations on a regular basis. Staff in these centers don't know the regulations, much less adhere to them. It is actually quite common for childcare centers to operate without following many of the regulatory rules. These are the same centers that do not put a significant effort into staff training, appropriate staff supervision, and correction where necessary.

Examples of routine violations include:

- ✓ Being out of ratio (having more children to a single staff member than is allowed)
- ✓ Staff members leaving rooms of children unattended
- ✓ Not sanitizing surfaces as required
- ✓ Not actively supervising children
- ✓ Talking or texting on cell phones while supervising children
- ✓ Not following nutritional requirements

Staff members who do not know the regulations will be much more apprehensive at a state inspection because they don't actually know the correct means of operation. In contrast, if the center operates on a daily basis according to the requirements, when the inspector walks in unannounced, they should be doing the right things and they will feel prepared. Having an inspector inside your center can make even the most confident staff members nervous, but being well prepared makes it less stressful.

How do you prepare your staff members for inspections? A full training curriculum should be part of your initial training process. Each employee needs to complete the full training, even if they have prior experience and even if your state regulations don't require it. Just because they worked in childcare does not mean they know the requirements. Just as it is common for some centers to not operate within the regulations, it is quite common for new staff members with prior experience in other facilities to have little knowledge of the state requirements for their job.

After initial training, you still have more training to complete. Providing initial training, does not guarantee all of the information was retained and put into practice. Sitting down and learning the rules must be combined with hands-on training and standard daily procedures. Reinforce the regulations every day. Correct as necessary and explain why. Tell the staff when they are violating a state regulation, even if the actual event doesn't seem very significant. Every staff member needs to know the rules, and work within those guidelines every day.

❖ Lesson From the Field: Teaching New Staff Members

I walked in on a relatively new staff member rewarding a class of toddlers with a handful of candy for each child. There were a few different violations on this simple act of rewarding children. The amount provided was way too much for each toddler and it was a food that was outside of the provided menus. I confirmed that the children had not washed their hands prior to having candy which is also a violation. Finally, the staff member had not washed her hands prior to serving food. It seems like a little thing and it wasn't an intentional violation, but if she had done this during an inspection it would have led to several citations.

This example opens up another important point of inspections and violations. When events occur that create a violation of rules, a single act can violate numerous rules. I've observed many times how one incident at a center was listed as numerous citations. This method is most often used when the event is significant, such as one that led to a child's injury or placed a child at risk. The inspector is likely to cite as many rules as she can find even when it all relates to one single error on the part of the center. When people review the violation history of the center, it looks like many bad things occurred rather than a single incident written up many times. This is another one of those areas where the inspector may have a great deal of flexibility to interpret.

Researching Inspection Reports

Another way to prepare for inspections is to keep on top of state citations in other centers. This is a fantastic way to research and learn about how to prevent violations in your own center. Most information regarding performance of childcare centers is public information. If your state maintains a website and publicly lists the results of inspections of childcare centers, you have a wealth of valuable information accessible with a few computer clicks. Routinely go to the website and look at the reports. Make note of trends in violations, these common violations may be repeated among centers for a couple of different reasons. These common mistakes may be things that are easily overlooked, such as paperwork errors or common daily practices. Another reason for many violations of the same mistake across numerous childcare centers, could be that the there is an emphasis by your state licensing department to look for this problem.

In addition, pay special attention to the citations noted for centers in your geographical area that are assigned to the same state inspector. State inspectors do a routine job and have habits just like the rest of us. You may see that your inspector is always looking for a few specific items along with the routine inspection. Knowledge is power! Doing the research and implementing the knowledge into your program will ultimately result in operating a more compliant childcare center with minimal violations.

❖ Lesson From the Field: High Chair Safety Straps

> *Our inspector would always check for safety straps on any high chair. It was a violation to have a child in a high chair without safety straps securing the child. She would also cite the center if safety straps were missing from the chair, even if there wasn't a child in the chair. It was predictable, we knew it ... and yet I still had that citation once as a safety strap was broken. It was hectic day and I took the strap off to fix it in a little while. That same day the inspector came and checked her routine items. We were cited for having a high chair without a safety strap even though there wasn't a child in the chair. I fixed and replaced it at the inspection. A violation was on the record but one that had a statement that it was "corrected at inspection."*

This inspection research is also valuable information for training your staff and helping them to understand the importance of their job in creating a safe and highly regarded childcare center. Sometimes this information is provided in a "shock value" format. As you read, you will find numerous violations that make you shake your head and say: "How could this happen?" Helping your staff understand can help to make sure those things don't happen in your center.

Staff training in my center regularly incorporated inspection reports that were posted on the state licensing website. Yes, we knew what was wrong with every center in our area and centers throughout the entire state. This helped keep my staff fully focused on things that could go wrong. It was for educational purposes. We used the information to better prepare ourselves and ensure our own compliance with the standards. I read many citations from all over the state. I paid closest attention to those of local centers as these gave us the best picture of what our own inspector was looking for when she visited us. It was very insightful into her perspective and what she would focus on during inspections.

State Inspections: What It's Really Like

When the inspector arrives, she should identify herself. As the manager of the center, you should handle the major parts of the inspection. It is your center and you are in charge. Confidence shows the inspector that you know what you are doing and that it is a well managed center. In your absence, you should always have someone who is qualified to take on this managerial role should there be a surprise inspection. An inspection can occur any time during operational hours. Handle the inspection and the inspector in a business like, matter of fact manner.

Answer all questions and use the following guidelines:

- ✓ Do not volunteer additional information
- ✓ Do not fill in silence gaps
- ✓ Do not chat about other things

Providing additional information can lead to more probing questions, and more attempts to find violations. Your inspector is not your adversary, but she is not your friend either. She is there to find any rules that are being broken and you are to provide the information required and shouldn't provide anything that is not specifically requested.

The inspector will most likely walk through the entire building observing classes, speaking with staff, and looking for any violations in operational practice. Teachers should respond pleasantly and answer questions from the inspector. Your staff should also be aware of the pitfalls of chatting with the inspector and providing more information than is required. In addition, extending conversations with inspector can create other problems when the teacher is supposed to be supervising the children. If the inspector takes your teacher's attention for too long, the children are likely to get "creative" with their activities. It is almost a guarantee that when small children believe no one is watching or correcting, the classroom behavior goes downhill quickly. Watch for this and be ready to step in as "teacher" while the staff member is questioned.

Even with the best of preparation, when you have a number of new staff members, mistakes can happen. This is simply due to the fact that these teachers haven't been on the job long enough to be fully prepared and competent in their work. It takes time for them to fully develop the skills and knowledge of the standards that impact the day to day care of children.

In addition to staff already being nervous about having an inspection, some inspectors will purposefully "drill" them making the situation even worse. The best you can do is prepare them for such realities so that they are better able to handle the situation.

❖ Lesson From the Field: State Inspector Tactics

I had an excellent reputation with our state licensing inspector. She was not friendly or personable. In fact, she was a stickler for detail and loved her rule book but we ran the center carefully and according to state standards and she knew it. Her first question was always "How many children do you have?" Knowing this I went through the building on a regular basis asking teachers how many children they had so they were always in practice. The funny result was that the children would often see me walk in and say "how many children do you have" or actually count and answer the question.

Another tactic that the inspector used was to "drill" the teachers on details, and take the position of "playing dumb" at times to make them explain things that she already knew. Despite this manner of inspection tactics, because the state representative was confident that we were complying with requirements and were a good place for children, we had very few inspections. In fact, I could predict the approximate time frame of our inspection because our inspector would do an "unscheduled" inspection approximately every 10 months. Other centers with the same inspector would see her many more times. Sometimes she would show up for unscheduled inspections multiple times within a single month. The number of inspections was correlated to the level of compliance with the state requirements. It was a nice benefit for managing a quality center which strictly adhered to state regulations.

❖ Lesson From the Field: Not Our Best Inspection

It was the end of the week and I was running a little later than usual as I headed out of the building to pick up school-age children from public school in my van. My teacher who drove the bus had already left for her afternoon route. As I headed out, I noticed a car pull up to the side of our building and park on the grass. I slowed my walk and tried to look to see if it was our licensing representative. It was that time of year. We were due for inspection. As she put her hand out and waved, I knew it was our inspector. I turned around and went back to the building. Ms. Seldon was coming out ... she saw the inspector and was ready to take my place on the van route. I handed her my keys and asked her to do the route so that I could manage the licensing inspection. The staff could do it, but it was easier on them for me to take charge of it.

After three years with no citations at all, this was not our year. The teachers answered all of her questions and it went well for the important details of supervision, ratio, and the care of children. She then wanted to sit down to write up the inspection report on her computer. I said I was going to layout afternoon crafts in the area where she was going to sit. She volunteered to go in the adjoining room. As she went in, she said: "What is this?" She pointed to some chipped paint on two closet doors. I explained that we had plans to paint the entire building the next year. We had put a great deal of money into the business that year ($20,000.00) to pay for two new air conditioning and heat systems and all new flooring. Paint was next on the list. As expected, she didn't care about the details ... she cited us for the chipped paint on the two doors.

Next, she wanted to see the van used for school-age transportation because it had just returned with the children. She looked in the van and asked for the list of children to be picked up. I carried a standard list every day and showed her that. Next, she wanted to see the first aid kit. That should have been easy; however, as she picked through the required items in the kit, the tweezers were missing. She cited us for tweezers and noted it as a "high risk" issue that tweezers were not in the first aid kit. Seriously, who determined that a lack of tweezers in the first aid kit related to a high risk to children? We didn't even use them due to the fact that the use of tweezers would create an invasive procedure ... those are left to parents.

She then looked at the fire extinguisher which I kept in the back of the van as a requirement. She said it needed to be secured and in the front of the vehicle. She wanted it secured between the front two seats. To her credit it was in the minimum standards that it be accessible to the driver. I had missed that detail so I asked her show it to me in the regulations, to which she replied: "I knew you were going to say that." As I often said, in the case of a fire, I would get the children out and I would not go back in for a fire extinguisher; therefore, the location wouldn't have mattered. However, it was in the standards and I had not placed it in the required location.

She gave us until Tuesday to have the fire extinguisher mounted inside the vehicle. She noted Wednesday as the deadline to have the doors completely repainted. My husband spent the entire weekend working on those details. I emailed her the pictures on Monday. I requested a response so that I could document it was complete. (Always keep your own set of records for verification.) We were done for another 10 months or so.

❖ Lesson From the Field: State Inspection with New Staff Members

This state inspection was on a Wednesday in January a few years later. The inspector was her usual "all business" self. She arrived at one of our most difficult times of day, transition time and bus run time (again). She seemed even more difficult than usual on this particular inspection. She first inspected the bus and the van for all applicable compliances related to transportation. She picked through the required items that must be in the van ... first aid kit supplies, fire extinguisher, list of children to be picked up, etc.

At this time one of my lead teachers left on the van run. My other lead teacher took the bus route. All of my experienced staff members were now either gone for the day or on the transportation routes. I was left to handle the inspection and keep three staff members with six months or less experience from making any mistakes that would result in a citation. The inspector did more standing around watching this time. It was as if she was just waiting to find something to write up.

After the children were woken from nap and lined up, they went into the kitchen for their snack. She checked the snack and tried to match it against the printed menu. With a full month of menus in front of her, the inspector wanted to see "this week's menu." I pointed to the current week on the menu. She wasn't able to understand where that day's menu was on a page with two weeks. Once I pointed to the week, she still couldn't find the actual snack for this time of day so I showed her exactly where it was.

She then turned her attention to the paperwork looking down and facing the kitchen preparation area. The new teachers had arranged children with 19 in one room and 8 in the other room. With a maximum staff to child ratio of 1:18 for 4 year olds, if they had simply moved one more child into the room with the younger children, it would have been acceptable to have only one teacher in the room with the children. However, due to their arrangement, I needed two teachers in one of the rooms.

During this time, one of the teachers went into the kitchen prep area for an extended time leaving the other teacher and me in the room with 19 children. Then the teacher in the room with me walked out of the room because a child in the restroom adjoining the dining area called to her. All the while the inspector was facing her papers and scrutinizing the menu. I stepped toward the bathroom door and used a hand gesture to say: "Get back in here!" She quickly moved back into the room satisfying the requirement of two staff in that room with 19 children.

The child in the bathroom came out to wash her hands in the adjoining dining room as they were required to do. The inspector began to question her as to whether she used soap or not. She told the inspector she did. The inspector asked again. The little girl repeated her answer. At this point I wasn't sure if she saw that the child hadn't used soap or if she was questioning our practices. (It is a standard practice for inspectors to question children in order to gain answers of center practices.) She looked at me and said the child needed to use soap when washing her hands. I knelt down and quietly asked the little girl if she had used soap and she shook her head. She was very nervous now and afraid of being in trouble with the stern stranger in the room. I quietly sent her back to wash her hands again and use soap. I wasn't sure if the inspector was going to use that as a violation or not.

Next, one new teacher passed a water pitcher to the other new teacher who loudly asked if it was "nasty." Really, was that an appropriate adjective for our drinking water? The first teacher correctly answered that it was left from lunch. Our practice was to pour out the water from earlier and refill it ... but it certainly wasn't nasty.

Finally, the inspector was ready to complete her paperwork and wrap up the inspection. She went into a small front room to complete the paperwork. She asked me to sign our inspection report on her computer screen. I had to verify that there wasn't a citation since I was signing but couldn't view the full report based on the way the program was laid out. She sarcastically said that she would tell me if there was anything on it; however, it was my right to verify the information before signing.

This is an example of why there should always be experienced people within the center. The experience and supervision not only provides the quality operations that are in full compliance of regulations but also allows for fast corrections into compliance when inexperienced staff members make mistakes. The work is hectic and there are many rules to remember. Over time, with experience these rules become second nature and just evidence themselves in how things are done.

❖ Lesson From the Field: Reserved Parking Spot

> *We are all creatures of habit. Our inspector would always park in the same place. Therefore, we learned to leave it open. We didn't allow anyone to park there. There was always an open place ready and waiting right in front of a big picture window in a classroom. The teacher in that classroom would make sure we knew that the inspector was there. Yes, we always tried to be in compliance and ready but it also doesn't hurt to know exactly when the inspector drives up and parks in front of your center.*

If you are following proper procedures, it doesn't mean that you do anything different. Just being aware that the inspector is there, is helpful. There is nothing like having an inspector in the building and teachers didn't realize it. Seeing her pull up provided about two minutes to let teachers know that an inspector was coming to visit them.

Final Routine Inspection Report

The inspector should show you the final report prior to you signing it. Make sure that you understand and agree with any violations of standards on the inspection report. There are a couple of possible areas where this may need further evaluation. If you are cited for something that you are not familiar with, have the inspector show you where it is in the licensing standards. It must be there if she is citing you for it. If you disagree with a report, you can state that on the form and still sign it.

There are means for objecting to items noted on a report and you will need to go through the proper channels if you disagree and feel that your objection is substantiated. As discussed earlier, you have the right to follow through with any citations that you feel are unsubstantiated. Just proceed with caution and tact since it is most likely that you will have to continue working with the same licensing representative.

Another possible consideration is that the inspector may be wrong. This often happens in paperwork. The required records can be quite cumbersome and files can become thick over time. As children stay with you for a number of years, these files can be "messier" to read. Children will have files updated and information added to them as it comes due at certain ages. Vaccination updates may wind up being on multiple pieces of paper. Some vaccinations will have a single vaccine and other have combination of vaccines in one dose. This can all get complicated when evaluating required records. Try to make sure that your files are in logical order and as organized as possible. Make it easy on the inspector to find the information. Even after doing all these things, if your inspector still says something is missing, verify it. Take the file and look! Make sure that she is correct. On numerous occasions, I found the information that the inspector couldn't find.

❖ Lesson From the Field: Verify any Recordkeeping Violations

During one inspection, our licensing representative was training another inspector. When it was time to scrutinize the files, our regular inspector took half of them and gave the other half to the inspector in training. The files are required to have very specific information. The trainee had seven items marked as not in the files. She told me each item and one by one after each item was stated, I went into the file and showed her the documentation. It is important to go and check when an inspector says something is missing from your file. I kept careful records, and most of the time it was in there. The inspector just wasn't able to locate it. If the inspector overlooks something and you don't show her where it is, then it is a deficiency even though the work was completed.

Receiving a Deficiency

Even with the best you can do, there will be times when you may not meet full compliance. Sometimes these things are beyond your control due to timing; parents who are remiss in getting their child's vaccinations; or other such situations. The inspector is usually not interested in "why" even if there are valid reasons. In those cases, you have to just fix the "deficiency" and move forward.

It is more likely that if you have a violation, you will agree with it. It was a mistake and you should correct it immediately. Then make sure it doesn't happen again. If the violation can be corrected while the inspector is still there, then you should do this. In Texas, violations must be documented as corrected after the inspection. There is a specific area to note if a violation was corrected at inspection. Obviously, the fact that you were able to immediately correct the violation is a nice note to your record.

There is no great shame in having a few small "paper work" type violations on your record; it happens. Frequently these errors occur because it is easy to miss a tiny detail here or there on paperwork simply due to the volume and complexity. You always want to strive to be in full compliance and be sure that your daily routine includes operating according to standards. With that being said, the minor violations noted that happen occasionally, are not likely to raise the attention of your licensing agency.

There are violations which truly stand out and can lead to severe consequences including having the inspectors visit very often to check up on you … or even the revocation of your license. These violations include things that would involve putting children at risk and most of these specifically relate to supervision issues. Supervision of children is arguably the most critical area of violations.

State Investigations: What It's Really Like

Investigations are different from routine inspections. Investigations are a result of a report or other occurrence at your center that was brought to the state licensing agency's attention. The investigator is most likely a different person and investigations will operate differently from routine inspections.

Reports can be obtained in two basic ways. Someone outside the center can file a report or a childcare center can file a "self-report" which lets the state agency know that something occurred which is required by licensing to be reported. Refer to your state regulations to determine which things must be reported to licensing. For the reports filed by someone outside of the center, you may never know who filed the report. It may be allowed to be filed anonymously or the state may require the person's name but will not share it with the center.

Certain situations may or may not be required to be reported, based on how the parent chooses to handle the situation. When minor injuries occur, parents can react in very different ways. If they choose to take the child to the emergency room or doctor due to an incident that occurred at your center, in Texas you are then required to report that to the state. The reality is some parents will take children to see the doctor for something very minor and others won't worry about it. The parent's choice in this case determines whether or not you would be required to file a self report. It is important to check back with the parent to see how the event was handled. That often means a phone call that evening after the center has closed to let them know you care about the child and it allows you to assess how the situation was handled and if it is necessary to file a self-report to the state.

❖ Lessons From the Field: Parent's View Impacts Investigation Potential

Here are just a few examples of parent reactions from the many minor things that happened to children in my years in the childcare business:

I called a mother to let her know that her three year old child had stuck a bead from an art project into his ear. (Our policy for safety was to never attempt to remove things that were embedded into the child's skin, ears, or nose.) She was very relaxed wanted to finish the activity she was in the middle of and would come at pick up time and get it out. The mother showed up at the regular scheduled time with a pair of tweezers. She went in with the tweezers and pulled the bead out of her child's ear.

A child put a tiny pebble from the outdoor playground into her ear. After my phone call to let them know, the divorced parents both arrived in separate cars and rushed the child to emergency room.

My all time favorite parent reaction was the following: An adorable two year old boy was leaning back in his chair and lost his balance. He not only fell back but hit his head on a commercial electrical outlet box. As head injuries often do, it bled a great deal! We called and his father arrived. He looked at the cut and said "We're going to put a spit wad on it and go ride the four wheeler."

In the case of a self-report, you are well aware that an investigation has been initiated and you can expect to see an investigator showing up at your door unannounced. The timing of how quickly the investigator appears will often be determined based on the perceived significance of the report. A report that appears to have placed children in danger, or a report of a significant injury, will likely result in a quick response and an investigation that happens very soon. If however, the state licensing department believes this is more of a routine occurrence, then it may take more time before the investigator shows up.

The time spent waiting can be very stressful. It is the proverbial "waiting for the ball to drop." You don't know when the investigator will show up and you are nervous about the possibility of being under investigation. If you have relevant information, go ahead and get it together in writing. Have it ready for when the investigator shows up. In addition, you can let your staff know that they will likely be questioned by the investigator if they were on duty or have knowledge of the incident.

An investigation does not automatically mean a violation. The investigator looks at all the evidence. She will talk to the staff members involved and evaluate the environment in which it happened. Depending on the incident, she may collect phone numbers of parents involved to verify information with them. This is where many of your parents will really stand up for you as they let the investigator know that it is a quality center. They will often confirm that the events were not due to a violation of standards in areas such as the environment or supervision. There is no substitute for a really well built relationship with parents.

On the other hand, if the report was not generated by the management of the center, you may not be aware that you are under investigation until the state investigator shows up. Anyone can file a report, and these can be based on real grounded information, insignificant information, incorrect information, or they can be totally falsified. It may have even been called in to the state because someone was angry with your center.

- ❖ Lesson From the Field: Sanitation Complaint

    Our first investigation involved a generalized complaint of sanitation violations. Essentially someone called the state and said we were "dirty." This wasn't triggered by any particular incident and so we didn't know who called it in.

    One day a car pulled up and a state investigator got out. She identified herself and let us know that someone had called in a sanitation complaint to the state. She was very cordial and spent some time walking through the center to see that it was well maintained, clean, and didn't have odors. She then observed diaper changing procedures; children washing hands at snack time; and other routine activities that were done according to standards. She was convinced that the complaint did not hold any merit and stated several times, "I don't know why they said the center was dirty." We later traced it back to an angry parent who chose to file a falsified complaint.

An investigation may include the state representative questioning some of the children. In the case above, the investigator pulled aside a couple of school-age children to ask them if they had to do things, such as wash their hands before they eat. When an investigator questions children, it can make them nervous and uncomfortable. The investigator will generally leave it up to you to talk to the parents and explain what happened. It is really not pleasant to have to explain to a parent why their child was used as a data source for a state investigation; especially when you haven't done anything wrong and the report was completely unsubstantiated.

Be careful who you trust and who has information. Limit your information on internal operations and management to your staff. Be careful what operational information is shared with parents and what your staff shares with others. Sometimes reports can come from disgruntled or former staff members. In many instances, you will be able to determine who filed the report. You will know what incident spurred the event or simply who is angry or acting irrational. Also, keep your ears open and listen to your staff when they suspect someone has filed a report. Sometimes what feels like rumors actually has substance. Being aware of such things means that you are prepared, such as the following example in which a former staff member filed a report months after leaving the center by her own choice.

❖ Lesson From the Field: Former Staff Initiate State Investigation

One investigation we had involved a former staff member who believed that I had provided a better "deal" to another staff member. The current staff member brought her infant with her for the 30 minutes prior to opening the center. Her babysitter would meet her and take the infant before the center ever opened. We were not licensed for infants at this time; therefore, the infant couldn't be in care when we were open. The former employee learned about the circumstances and called in a complaint to the state licensing agency. She stated that we were keeping infants even though we were not licensed for that age group. Keeping your eyes and ears open is always a good thing. A valued staff member told me this complaint had been filed. I found it hard to believe as this person had been a good employee and left the center on great terms and by her own choice.

However, when the vehicle pulled up and the state investigator got out, we all knew that it was true. We were ready for this one. We answered questions and showed her around the center so that she could verify we weren't "hiding any infants" (my words not the investigator's comments). We told the investigator exactly what our procedures were for the staff member's infant that did come to the center in the morning but was gone before she opened the center for the day. We were once again cleared of any wrong doing following the investigation.

There are incidents where you know a parent is very angry and their best recourse, whether it is justified or not, will be to file a report with the state. When you know that you have an angry parent or a major incident has occurred, prepare for the investigation. Make a full documentation folder of all of the facts surrounding the incident. Include written statements from staff members involved in the incident. If it involves an injury, take pictures. Be straight forward and factual. Make sure that you express this to your staff members as they write down their account of the situation. This is not the time to be dramatic or emotional; it is not appropriate to include negative statements regarding the parent or child. Keep it professional.

Make a copy of the file documents. File the original documents away in your private files that are locked away. Have the set of copies ready in case an investigator shows up. These can be difficult times as you wait from day to day wondering if a state investigator will be showing up or not. These types of things are out of your control. Your best solution is simply to "get your ducks in a row" and be ready if it happens. For our "big one" of all incidents, see the Schoenherr Incident in Chapter 17.

Thankfully, extreme incidences and extreme behaviors such as this example are very rare but it is important to include. When you are dealing with so many different individuals and personalities, things can happen which are extreme and having the knowledge of such examples will help you to manage your own extreme circumstances with more confidence and professionalism.

5

Children's Safety

In this chapter, you will discover the complex elements of safety and how to insure children's safety through policies, procedures, and supervision including:

- Overview of Safety
- Procedures for Dropping Off and Picking Up Children
- Release of Children
- Indoor Environment Safety
- Outdoor Environment Safety
- Safety Supervision
- Safety at Parties and Special Events
- Children with Special Needs
- Handling Emergencies
- Responsibility Extends Past Your Center

Overview of Safety

The safety of the children in your care is the absolute most important focus of childcare. It is more critical than regulations, paperwork, education and all else. Children must be safe and well cared for inside a healthy environment. Caring for children well is a wonderful profession and provides a positive impact on the lives of children and their parents. In contrast, caring for children poorly is unacceptable and can literally put children's lives in danger! Childcare should never be entered into as "just a business investment." Decisions must be based first on care and second on the "bottom line." It requires your heart, as well as your full commitment to the safety and well-being of the children in your care.

Procedures for Dropping Off and Picking Up Children

Children should always be walked all the way into the building by a parent and taken into care by a staff member. Parents should be required to personally sign their child in each day as they transfer the responsibility of care from themselves to the center.

- ❖ Lesson From the Field: Dropping off Children

    One citation incident involved a center that was cited for not reporting to the state that a child was wondering around for some time prior to coming into the center. The parent had dropped the child off at the door and the child chose to wander away from the building. No one on staff knew the child was there. The center was cited for not reporting the incident ... not for a supervision issue. The parent was clearly at fault for not insuring the child had entered the center and been taken into care before leaving.

You can prevent this type of safety problem at your center by requiring the parents to bring the child into the center and personally handing over the care to the teachers on duty. It sounds like something that should obviously be a part of the policies and daily routine, but parents vary greatly in their personalities and supervision. Some will not see a problem with opening the car door, letting the child out, and driving away.

Release of Children

Release policies are a very important topic. You must have a written release policy and your staff must know what that is. This is a very real safety issue that must be strictly enforced to ensure that you do not allow a child to go home with someone who is not authorized to take him. Most centers have a written list of individuals allowed to pick up a child. If you don't know the individual who arrives to pick up a child; you must verify the identification (generally the driver's license) and make sure that she is on the list of authorized people for that child.

Unauthorized individuals will at times show up to pick up a child. Usually this is because the parents didn't think anything about sending someone to pick up their child. These parents completely forget that every detail must be handled carefully and that each person picking up a child must be on the authorized list. Having an unauthorized person show up to pick up children happens relatively often, especially when the parents have unexpected emergencies. If someone arrives to pick up the child but is not on the list, you must not release the child until you have verified that the parent sent them. This can be very uncomfortable. Some people will understand why you won't release the child. Others will be very angry over the situation. The child probably even knows the person well; often it is a family member. Just because the child knows the person does not mean she has permission to take the child. This is how kidnapping incidents can happen. Stick to careful policies and procedures. Your responsibility is to keep the child safe. Keep the children safe and keep your center off of the local news reports.

Prepare your staff to handle such situations. Share potential problematic situations, review state citations, and review legal issues in childcare with your staff. Always have someone on duty who is able to handle the management of the center and can carry out difficult tasks. In addition to training your staff, make sure that the director is always available by phone if not on site. The staff should be able to call the director and get input if they are not sure how to handle a particular situation. Have your staff enforce your rules and policies; then back them up.

Custody issues are another important safety topic. If it happens to be an ugly separation, it can get very sticky because while caring for the child, in many cases, you will be caught in the middle of the parents' disputes. You cannot keep a child from a parent, unless you have court documents that show the parent does not have custodial rights. Put a question on your enrollment paperwork asking if there are legal custody papers filed for the child. If there are legal documents filed, you must have a copy of the court documents. You must know what legal issues surround the child in order to fully comply with those custody orders.

Another safety area to mention is that of evening care, particularly when that care is provided on Saturday nights such as a parents' night out. There are situations where there are not any good outcomes and you must make a choice. An example would be a parent who shows up drunk to pick up a child. It is clearly not safe for the child to leave with the parent; however, refusing to release a child to a custodial parent can put you in an extremely difficult situation. On the other hand, allowing the child to go with an intoxicated parent could place you at great liability if something were to happen to the child. Circumstances like these will put you in a no win situation. There is no good way out but you have to choose one of the options. My advice is to always choose the child's safety, even if it requires involving the police department.

Indoor Environment Safety

As the manager, it is your job to create and maintain a safe environment for the children in your care. Establishing a safe center begins with the basics of classroom layouts and procedures, along with the right choice of toys and educational materials. Also, take care to insure that all chemicals and hazardous materials are stored properly and locked away ... far from the reach of small hands.

Take care when choosing shelving units that there are no sharp edges. Also insure that the units are stable and do not pose a tipping hazard. One heavy shelf falling over on a small child can cause significant injury. Be sure that the children's toys and materials you select are safe and do not contain things such as: sharp edges which can cut; magnets which can be ingested; lead based paints; or other hazards. Also, ensure that materials are age appropriate. Children under three years old should not have access to toys, educational materials, or art supplies with small parts due to the risk of choking. A well managed childcare center provides a safer environment than many settings because of the regulations and care that goes into an environment designed just for children.

Know the children in your center. Even though the most often stated age for children to be allowed access to small pieces is three years old, there are many three year olds who still have a tendency to put things in their mouths. Many good toys and educational materials have small parts. The materials provided should be carefully chosen for the particular group of children. The children's ages are only a guideline. When is it appropriate to allow children smaller materials? In larger centers, classrooms or groups of children could be determined based on such developmental stages. This allows children who are ready more access to the smaller materials while keeping others from working with them. In smaller centers, it may be more difficult with fewer classrooms. In these centers, it may be necessary to separate children into groups inside of a classroom. Another option is to delay adding these items until all of the children in the classroom have moved past the stage of putting tiny objects in their mouths, ears and noses.

❖ Lesson From the Field: Small Pieces and Small Children

I've seen many instances of children in my own center who were "old enough" by standards for small materials and yet would still place small items inside their ears, noses, or mouths. It is very common. This is particularly true of small beads ... for some reason these seem very tempting to try out if you are three years old. On some occasions, we could see and reach the items or have a child blow their nose and get an object out. It was my policy to never go into an ear, nose, or deep in the mouth to retrieve an item. At this point, you have to be concerned with pushing it further inside or creating an injury.

Some children are much more prone to this type of behavior. Watch them closely or remove them from areas and projects with small pieces. If you do find that a child has placed a small bead or other object inside his ear, nose, or mouth, then you should notify the parent. The next step belongs to her. She may choose to come and try to get it out. Often this works well. Remember a parent is allowed to go "dig" inside and pull something out while it's best that the center staff not attempt such actions. The parent may choose not to do this, or the item may be too deep and require a trip to the doctor's office or emergency room.

If a child has swallowed a small object, then it is important to contact the parent. Often there is really nothing that can be done. If the object was tiny it will generally just pass through the system. Always call the parent to make the determination as to the next step. It is the parent's choice on how to proceed.

Learning activities, toys, and art supplies must all be selected carefully. Pay attention to ages and accessibility to small objects as well as individual personalities in children. Research safety recalls of children's products on a regular basis. Remove any recalled items from your center. If children are allowed to bring toys from home, pay careful attention to what they bring and any hazards associated with those toys.

❖ Lesson From the Field: Spinning Toys

We would have play days on occasions such as spring break and some fun summer days where the children brought their own toys to share with friends. On one such occasion a child brought a toy with a spinning part. It was a popular toy and didn't appear to be anything concerning; however, the spinning part got too close to one of the girl's long hair and spun the hair up into a big mess. The staff wasn't sure what to do and even contemplated cutting it out. The parent was called to fix it and was very angry. From that point on, we didn't allow toys with spinning parts and of course the staff was told they were not to cut a child's hair. This falls under those circumstances that can be viewed very differently depending on the particular parent. Parents should be called and make those decisions as well as be the one to cut hair if anyone does it.

Parent's responses will be very different. Some will appear to be very angry, upset, or scared and other parents will take these minor incidences all in stride. You will get to know your parents. Then you know which ones need a call for every scratch and which ones only need a note at the end of the day. Take care to document every incident and have the parent sign the form ... no matter how small the boo-boo. This will make sure the parent is notified of the incident. The procedure also ensures that there is a connection between caregivers in case the one who witnessed the incident has gone for the day. Lastly, it provides a documentation should there be concerns that happen later. It doesn't happen often, but there may be a parent who comes back angry later, or files a report to the state at a later date. The documentation allows you to refer back to the specific details of the event. In addition, written documentation which is accurately described, dated, and signed provides a better stance for your business in the case of liability issues.

Cleaning safety is very important as daily operations include a great deal of cleaning. Tables must be cleaned before and after each meal or snack; hard floors must be mopped; trash taken out; bathrooms cleaned; and carpeted floors must be vacuumed. Cleaning must be handled with great care. In order to maintain a clean center, these things must be done repeatedly throughout the day which means cleaners will be taken out of their storage areas. Staff must be carefully trained in how this cleaning is done while children are in care.

The children should not be near the cleaners at any time. It is best to train your staff to not set cleaners down at all. If these cleaners have to be sat down, then the items must be set on a high shelf so that they can't be reached by children. The problem with setting them down, just for a minute, while the staff member is cleaning is that the cleaners can then be easily forgotten. It only takes one employee forgetting to put the cleaner away for it to be found and potentially ingested by a child. In addition to policies and procedures, staff must be supervised. Some will still make those mistakes that you have trained and guarded against.

- ❖ Lesson From the Field: Bleach Water

    Even with all the training and procedures I put into place, on a few occasions, I would still find the "bleach water" (our cleaner of choice for most jobs) left down. It was rare, but when it happened I proceeded to find out who did it. I reinforced to the individual that she didn't follow the procedures and therefore, was potentially putting children at risk. I only allowed one bottle of bleach water. That was my method of keeping track of it so that each staff member used the same bottle and if it was missing it was immediately known and had to be located. Although this may not be practical in very large centers, it was a very effective control method in my center.

Cleaners left down are dangerous! This is where it is the manager's job to know what is going on and to actively be in classrooms and around the building supervising staff members. Ultimately, the one in charge is responsible for the actions of staff members.

Also take care that there are no buckets for mop water or other cleaners down in areas where children have access. Small children can drown in a bucket of mop water! Cleaning should be done when children are not in the area; all cleaning materials should be promptly removed and areas dry before children are allowed back into them.

Diaper changing has elements that create safety concerns. The traditional diaper changing table is on a raised surface to make it easier for the staff members to change the child's diaper. This can cause a safety concern as children may fall. Busy wiggling children placed on a table above the floor need to have the safety straps utilized. An even better choice that I highly recommended is the use of very simple and inexpensive floor diaper changing pads. These are simply placed on the floor and the child can't fall off of them. It does mean that the person changing the diaper must bend down and get on the floor, but it is a good trade off for safety. It also means that the person changing the diaper isn't required to pick up the child; this can be difficult as some children are very heavy as they get older and still require diaper changing. A final advantage to the floor diaper changing pad is that it can be put away and stored between diaper changes rather than being out in the open in the room. Raised diaper changing tables can become a hazard. Young children may climb on them and fall, or knock the table over onto themselves or other children. There are numerous citations posted where children were injured from such occurrences.

Whatever diaper changing method you choose, be sure to refer to your states requirements for sanitizing the diaper changing pad. It needs to be sanitized between each child. Also provide gloves and require hand washing between each diaper change; this insures that there is no transference of germs between children. Texas standards also require each child to have his hands washed after diaper changing. Diaper changing sounds simple, but when applying all of the regulations, safety procedures, and performing all of this on multiple children numerous times a day, it can be a very time consuming task.

❖ Lesson From the Field: Unbelievable Things You Have to Evaluate

I was told that Melanie's BM looked like it had ants in it and that there were ants in her bag. I put on the gloves and had to open up the diarrhea diaper (overwhelming smell and all) and check for contents. It looked odd but no absolute on the "ant" theory so I told them to keep an eye on it.

This was not an isolated incident, there are numerous times when you are required to have conversations with parents about their child's bodily functions that can include more detail than you really would like. It's not unusual to have to check a toilet to see if a child who is already potty trained has diarrhea. Other times you will need to evaluate what is on the floor, toilet, diaper, or other surface. You may need to determine: "Is it a spill, vomit, feces, etc.?"

Children's Safety

The dress code for children at your center should focus on what is best for the children, particularly in reference to safety issues. Many clothing items that may be cute and fun such as flip flops, dangling earrings, and necklaces are not good choices for children in care.

Items to consider in your dress code include:

- ✓ Wear comfortable inexpensive play clothes for running outside and doing arts and crafts indoors
- ✓ Shoes with backs to support feet and help prevent falls
- ✓ No necklaces, or have the teachers remove them before outdoor play (these can pose a choking hazard if caught on playground equipment outdoors)
- ✓ No dangling earrings which can be pulled by other children and cause injury
- ✓ No expensive jewelry since items will get lost on occasion

If children come to the center wearing prohibited items, take those items and bag them up for the child to take home. Gently explain to the child "why" these things should not be worn to school and that you are going to put them into their cubby or backpack to take home. This is important; the child understands that you are not taking and keeping their prized items. You are simply saying these are not safe to have at school and you will send them home.

Naptime safety includes selecting cots or mats that conform to all your state requirements. In addition, only age appropriate bedding should be used. This is a particular concern for children under two years old who may have moved up from the baby bed and onto a mat.

Take care when it comes to the naptime details including the following:

- ✓ Safe and age appropriate sleeping materials
- ✓ A state approved mat or cot for each child
- ✓ Leaving space for teachers to walk to each child without stepping over children
- ✓ Don't block fire exits with sleeping mats, cots, or other items
- ✓ Leave adequate lighting to supervise the children
- ✓ Make sure that the teachers can see every child while they are resting
- ✓ Have your state required number of teachers supervising the children
- ✓ Have teachers move around the room and actively supervise resting children

Naptime is not "break time" for the staff on duty. It is very important that the children are well supervised during this time period just as in the other times of day. There must be the correct number of staff caring for the children and actively supervising. Have your staff members walk around and check on the children as they are resting. During this time, children can have difficulties with breathing if they have colds or allergies. In addition, I've witnessed children pull pebbles, money, or toys out of their pockets and put them in their mouths at naptime. (Treasures collected that were saved for later.) Staff should be aware of each child in their care and monitor the room carefully throughout naptime.

Administering medications is a choice for the center. You can choose not to administer medicine or agree to do so. Many children will need medicine while in care from time to time and some children will need medicine daily; choosing not to administer medicine may impact enrollment. Keep in mind that an additional degree of responsibility is added when you are administering medication. Make it clear in your policies the requirements for administering medication. The center should follow all state regulations regarding such procedures.

These procedures will generally include:

- Having parents sign medicine in on an official form
- Making sure over the counter medicine is appropriate for the age of the child
- Verifying medicine has not expired
- Getting replacements if medicine, kept at the center, for the child has expired
- Only administering the specified amount of medicine based on the child's age or weight as stated on medication instructions or as prescribed by a doctor
- Documenting each time medicine is provided and who administered the medication

In order to have better accuracy in providing medication, it is best if this duty is assigned to a specific person. Often this would be the director or assistant director. In addition, you may want to specify when medications will be given. This helps to create a regular schedule that can be followed each day; otherwise, you may be administering medicine at many different times throughout the day. Without a set schedule, the likelihood of forgetting a particular dosage time is increased. At my center, I specified medicine would only be provided at lunch and afternoon snack times. It makes sense for most medications as they can be given by the parent in the morning and the center would provide midday administrations. The parents could then provide any evening doses after the children were picked up.

Topical medications include diaper rash creams, antibiotic creams, lotions for dry skin or skin conditions, and other such medicines that are placed on the skin. Administration of these medicines, in some cases, may require all of the same procedures including signing the medicine in and documenting its use. In other instances, state regulations for topical medications may note that a parent providing such a medicine is giving "implied permission" and it doesn't require the same level of documentation. In either case, for the center's own records and liability protection, it is best to have written permission on file and to document each time the medicine is used. In addition, do not apply creams or ointments that have not been expressly approved by the parent. Even using what may seem like the most basic topical ointment, such as an antibiotic ointment applied to a scraped knee, a specific child may have an allergic reaction to the medicine.

Keeping electrical outlets covered sounds like such an easy detail; yet keeping this done seems to be a common ongoing problem. There are numerous citations in almost any review of state documents which substantiate the problem of uncovered outlets. Teachers will do something as simple as vacuum a room and not replace the cover. It is an important supervision concept: Every time you walk into a room, check for overall environmental safety including making sure all electrical outlets are covered. Exposed outlets can injure small children as they complete their "science explorations" by seeing what happens when you "stick" things into the sockets.

In addition, pay special attention to cords connected to outlets. It is best to have all cords out of the reach of children and secured so that these do not pose a tripping hazard. In addition, make sure that there is nothing heavy or dangerous attached to the other end of that cord which could fall on a child if the cord was pulled.

Doors can lead to injury if care is not taken in how doors are designed and operated. Even under the best of circumstances, you can wind up with the occasional smashed finger in a door.

❖ Lesson From the Field: Doors and Injuries

Two year old Nelson always wanted to play with the door to his classroom and the doorstop. The door had hinges that hooked into the doorstop on the bottom to secure the door open. On one particular day, he was doing it again. While pushing it, he severely smashed his pinky finger in the doorstop. It looked like a cut in the shape of a "c" taking up most of his top finger pad on his right hand.

I started down the list of emergency contact numbers. I wasn't able to reach his mother at any of the numbers provided for her. Next, I started calling his father's numbers. I left messages at the numbers provided. Finally, his father returned the call. I explained the situation and injury. He said: "Maybe he will quit playing with the door now." I agreed sometimes lessons are tough. He said that he would just look at it when he got there and thanked me for the call. The injury healed up rather quickly.

These are real concerns; injuries can be far worse than pinched or bruised fingers. There are even incidences of fingers being cut off when trapped inside the back hinge area of doors. Create procedures to help with such safety issues. Policies such as keeping children away from doors while in the classroom can reduce such injuries. Also, there are safety products which can be used within a childcare center including products to keep doors from injuring fingers. Take care in evaluating safety and put into place all of the safety measures you can to prevent injuries.

Purses are another hazard. It seems like a minor thing and yet it can be a real concern in childcare centers. You don't know what is in a purse. There could be medicines, sharp objects, and other hazards that curious little hands and minds would like to explore. Ensure staff members know they are supposed to keep their purses out of reach of the children. Then as you make your routine walk through of rooms, be sure to look for this detail. There are other hazards in some centers' classrooms which simply don't need to be there. The following is just such an example:

❖ Lesson From the Field: Unnecessary Hazards

A center with a good reputation had an incident regarding scented air fragrance oil in the classroom. The container of scented oil was left down at "child level" in a toddler classroom. As toddlers do, the child investigated the oil … with his mouth. He "ingested" the fragrance oil. The striking reality is that the situation could have been even worse as the deficiency stated that the "burner and oil" were immediately removed from the classroom.

Diligent safety procedures must include no candles, no scented oils, and no hot drinks (such as coffee). These are not necessary and can present hazards to children. Eliminate these items from the children's rooms then accidents involving them won't happen.

Outdoor Environment Safety

More injuries seem to happen in the outdoor environment than any other. It is not because the outdoor is more hazardous as such. It is because the children are more free and active. Outdoor time is very important; it allows the children to just be children. This includes running, active play, and being louder than is appropriate indoors. This freedom and activity means that children are more likely to get hurt.

The outdoor environment must be carefully established in order to prevent accidents as much as possible. All of the fences and latches must be in good repair. The outdoor ground should be well maintained and a responsible staff member should evaluate the outdoor space prior to every time the children enter it.

What is that teacher evaluating? The outdoor space should be evaluated for things like appropriate temperature (too hot or cold); stray animals that could have wandered into the yard; and anything else that may stand out. In some times of year, it is common to have excessive insect activity such as ants, mosquitoes, and bees. Check your grounds prior to every time children go outside to play. This can mean numerous checks each day. It's worth all the effort to keep your children safe.

❖ Lesson From the Field: Check the Playground Every Time

This example came from a health inspector years ago relaying what he had seen at one time in his work. He had been to a childcare center that had a dead bat in the yard. As he stated, someone had checked the grounds and didn't let the children go outside; however, if they had let the children outside it could have led to some severe consequences.

Fences are an important part of your outdoor playground. Fences should be kept in good condition. As with all maintenance in a childcare center, this is a constant process. Children can be rough on your fencing and repairs are often part of regular maintenance.

Chain link fences provide a climbing wall in a child's eyes. This can cause a means to "escape," injuries to the child, and damage to the fence. Make sure children are well supervised and not allowed to climb the fence. Wood fences have their own set of challenges. This type of fence can leave splinters in children's fingers. Wood fences can deteriorate over time and need pickets replaced. You may also find that as the fence becomes weaker, it is an even greater temptation for children to kick and even knock out pickets.

The playground toys that you choose should be carefully considered prior to purchasing them. There are a number of inexpensive playground toys that provide lots of good fun and don't pose obvious hazards. Some great options are sand tables, bubble tables or tubs, and play structures of different varieties. Play structures come in many forms including houses, boats, and cabins. Climbing toys can provide great opportunities for large motor development in children. Careful consideration should be used when choosing climbing toys. The higher the climber reaches into the air, the greater a potential fall. Smaller children should only have access to smaller scale climbers in order to reduce the risk of injury due to their small size and their less developed physical skills.

❖ Lesson From the Field: Outdoor Climbers and Injuries

Even with a relatively small outdoor climbing structure, I had children get up on the top and fall onto the "use zone." (The use zone is a designated area surrounding outdoor toys with material designed to lessen the impact of a fall.) One incident included a child that got his leg stuck between plastic railings that were actually very close together. These incidences only resulted in little scratches but still demonstrate the reality of how easily injuries can occur even with the best planned materials.

There are commercial grade toys which usually last well but are very expensive. Good choices for outdoor equipment are the commercial grade toys that are stationary. These include small scale climbers along with fire trucks and school bus toys that have springs on the bottom and bounce. Be careful which ones you invest your money in, as these can cost well over a thousand dollars for a single toy! It can be really frustrating to have to get rid of expensive toys because you find these pose a high risk of injury.

❖ Lesson From the Field: Outdoor Toys that Contribute to Injuries

I had to take away a number of expensive commercial toys that looked like such fun for children. The toys were fun for the children ... too much fun in many instances. These toys included a stationary bike which held six children who road in a circle. What can that hurt? They road so fast it was very dangerous to others. Other children wanted on and the children riding in circles would run into them or over their feet. Another hazard was that when a child's foot came off the pedal as the toy was moving fast in a circle, that pedal was still spinning rapidly and could hit his leg and cause an injury. It posed too much of a hazard and was removed from the playground.

Another toy that provided great fun was a little bucket type toy that children sat in and turned the middle wheel to make it spin. (Picture the teacup ride at Disneyworld.) Children used it wildly and it repeatedly made them sick or they bumped their chins and heads inside because it was spinning so quickly and they were very dizzy.

One more toy that I had removed from my playground was a large "see saw" type toy with four seats spaced out in a square that allowed children to bounce up and down independently on springs (not connected to the other riders). They would bounce so wildly that they would come completely off the seats; fall off the toy onto the ground; and also hit other children who wondered too close to the bouncer.

Children don't do much in moderation, and as discussed earlier, the outdoor playtime is when children are allowed the most freedom to be active. This should definitely be considered as you choose outdoor toys. When choosing playground equipment with movement, think carefully about how that piece will fit into your very busy playground; filled with active children running, chasing balls, and not necessarily watching what is going on around them.

Your front porch and steps should be carefully maintained and evaluated for safety. This is the primary place for children to be dropped off and to leave the center in the evening. Evaluate not only how it is on a beautiful sunny day, but how it functions when it is pouring down rain or snowing? Make sure the steps, rails, and walkways don't become slippery and hazardous for parents and children.

Other outdoor areas which need careful consideration with respect to safety include your front lawn and driveway as well as all the other property surrounding your building which is not part of the children's outdoor play space. Depending on your location, you may find that there are dogs in your yard or a neighbor's cat has wondered onto your property. These animals need to be somewhere other than your front yard. As the responsible person for the children and families who are coming to your center, it is your job to take care of these animals which don't belong.

❖ Lesson From the Field: Stray Animals

I found that I had to deal with loose or stray pets quite a few times over the years. As someone who loves animals, I found myself going to extreme measures at times to get the dogs and cats that came my way to an appropriate home. Some were pets and owners had to be located. Others were homeless animals that wandered onto the property or were dumped off there. On some occasions, I had parents who took them home and on a couple of occasions I took them in and found homes ... and one rescued cat still lives with my family today. How you handle the stray and displaced animals is a choice, but you must see that they are removed from your center quickly and that they are not accessible to the children in your care.

The driveway is another area of concern. This is where you really feel how far your responsibility spreads out. Yes, you are the one who is responsible for correcting the behavior of the parents who drive too fast or otherwise recklessly in your driveway! This can be a touchy situation. You may see it yourself, or you may have other parents reporting incidences of reckless driving to you. You will need to contact the offending parent and express your concern about the safety of the driveway. If that parent still drives reckless, you may need to take further action, even to the point of having him withdraw his child from your center. It sounds extreme, but it's a real area of concern when there are many small children getting in and out of cars in your driveway.

Parents are often in a hurry when dropping off their children and when they are picking them up. When parents get in a hurry, sometimes they do things without the full awareness of safety that you have as you operate a childcare center.

❖ Lesson From the Field: Driveway Safety

I had a number of parents who would drive through the yard if the front drop off circle didn't move fast enough. There were obvious tire tracks through the front yard and this let others know the "alternate pathway" if they wanted to speed up the drop off process. It was necessary to put out parent notes and post a notice on the front door stating: "Please do not drive through the yard when dropping off your children." This was damaging to the property and more important it created a hazard for parents and children who were exiting their cars and trying to come into the center.

It is necessary to let parents know when their actions are creating a hazard for children. If you don't say anything, it will continue. Just as in the example of driving through the yard, it will increase as others follow. Not correcting implies it is acceptable.

Safety Supervision

Remember everything that goes on within the walls of your center is your responsibility. The supervision of staff, children, facilities, and programs should be constantly assessed through hands-on managing of the center. This means getting out of the office and really knowing what is going on throughout the building. Supervise and correct teachers, especially when their actions, or lack thereof, could lead to safety concerns for children. This is discussed much more in Chapter 13: Staff Supervision. From a safety perspective, it is important to make sure that children are carefully supervised at all times. Some children will walk out of their classroom and on a rare occasion you will have that challenging child who attempts, or even succeeds in running out of your building. (Fire codes usually state that all fire exists must remain unlocked during business hours which can contribute to the potential problem.) At that moment, there had better be a teacher there supervising and ready to stop the child from running out of the building.

❖ Lesson From the Field: Children Who Try To Run Away

Over the years, I had more children's behaviors that needed careful and immediate correction, than I can even begin to count. I had one child run out of the building! The wonderful teacher in the room yelled for help in her room and ran after him and brought him back inside the building. I've had children try, and yes sometimes succeed in going under the wooden playground fence. I've had a child work through double latches on the exterior of the fence and get out, again he was caught. I've had a small group of children kick through a wood fence to try to get out of the playground. Due to the careful supervision of teachers, none of these resulted in anything more than some disciplinary action, playground repairs, and behavior reports to parents.

Near closing time, some managers will allow one staff member to be there alone. This is not advisable. There should always be two teachers available, even when there is only one child left at the end of the day. This is for the safety of the child, or children in care, and for the benefit of the teachers. As always, with small children you never know when an emergency might occur.

- ❖ Lesson From the Field: Accidents Can Happen At Any Time

    One of our more significant injuries occurred near closing time. Two teachers were supervising one remaining child at the center. The child walked across the room and tripped over his own little feet. He went head first into a toy shelf. His forehead was cut against the shelf (which had rounded edges – not sharp). The force of the fall led to the head injury which gashed his forehead to the point his skull was visible. With two teachers there, one was able to administer first aid while the second teacher made emergency phone calls to the parent and to me. I arrived shortly. I drove the parent and child to the emergency room where the child was given stitches and recovered very well. Had there been only one teacher, this would have been an even more difficult situation.

Safety at Parties and Special Events

As you open your doors to family and friends for parties, graduations, and other special events, you must take even more care in safety. At these times you fill your center with many more people. Most of the parents, grandparents, and other visitors are not conscious of all that goes into creating a safe environment. Purses are often left down where children have access to them. Small visiting children of family members may run loose and get into things or parents may put an infant carrier with the baby inside on the floor.

- ❖ Lesson From the Field: Visitors and the Safety of Children in Your Care

    Parents and grandparents would bring in purses and lay them on the floor not thinking anything of the hazard this could create for small children. I would simply pick them up and let them know that I was going to put the purses on a high shelf so the children wouldn't have access to them.

    It was my little world and I was responsible for all the lives that entered. I took that knowledge very seriously. I never minded correcting those outside who were just not that familiar with it. They never seemed to mind that I moved their things. Even if they had minded, my responsibility was to the safety and care of the children, not to have everyone happy with me.

- ❖ Lesson From the Field: Visitors, Supervision, and Regulations

    I watched many times as parents of preschool age children brought in tiny babies with them for parties and at times set them on the floor in their carriers. There were so many children and adults that this clearly posed a safety issue for the child left on the floor.

    I also watched on other occasions as parents came into the center. They would often set their infants in carriers on the floor and walk out of the room leaving the babies completely unattended. Solutions for such situations would include picking up the infant and taking her to the parent, or having a staff member stay with the child. Even if the child is not enrolled, you do not want your state inspector to walk through and see an unattended child. Even more important, you don't want anything to happen to an infant left on the floor in a world full of busy toddlers and preschoolers.

Children with Special Needs

Special needs can vary widely. These can be as simple as dietary changes or as complex as physical or mental disabilities. If you have children in care with special needs, make sure that your staff has appropriate training on how to handle those needs. Training may also include how to use special devises such as monitoring equipment for the safety of the child. We discuss more on special needs in Chapter 16: Children's Behaviors.

❖ Lesson From the Field: Knowledge of Special Equipment

One recent review of licensing citations included a note that the staff on duty in a childcare center did not have training and knowledge of a child's special needs. The staff did not know how to use the special monitoring equipment for the particular child; therefore, creating a potential safety concern for that child.

Handling Emergencies

No matter how hard you work to create a safe environment and good supervision, when you are caring for many small children there will be accidents and minor injuries. These can happen even within the best of circumstances. As stated before, always document every incident no matter how minor and have a parent sign the incident report. Check to see if your state agency has a standardized form to use. If there is not one available online from your state regulatory agency, you can create your own.

Having the form signed provides documentation that the parent was notified and provides a record of the communication for the center. The incident report alone is acceptable for all those little boo-boos and minor bumps and bruises. Anything more dramatic should result in both an immediate phone call to the parent as well as the signed incident report.

First aid kits should remain completely stocked and readily available. Check your licensing regulations for a complete list of what is required to be kept in them. The specifications of the first aid kits can also be part of a routine inspection and missing items can result in a violation on your inspection report. Check the kits often for expiration dates of products and refill items as needed. Let your staff know the importance of not removing items from the first aid kit without replacing them. It seems the easiest item to go missing from it is the thermometer. It is taken out often to evaluate children's health. It is very easy for teachers who are busy with children to set it down rather than return it. The same is true for consumable items inside the first aid kit. If a teacher using one of the first aid kits notices that it is low on bandages or she takes the last one, she should notify the director so that the materials can be purchased and the kit promptly replenished.

Parents should be informed as soon as possible, when an injury occurs. Let the parent know exactly what happened and to the best of your knowledge the extent of the injury. There are numerous examples of how, in only a moment, a small child can have an accident which requires medical care. The following is one such example:

- ❖ Lesson From the Field: Children's Behaviors and Accidents

    A three year old child climbed up onto a chair for a better view of something through the window. When he was asked to get down, instead of stepping down, he jumped down. He landed on a toy storage box, lost his balance, and fell into a wooden storage unit. This left a significant cut on his forehead. It required his parent to come and take the child to the doctor for stitches.

If the injury is significant and requires more than simple first aid, your policy should require the parent to come to the center and personally evaluate the injury. The parent should be the one to decide if the child needs medical treatment; should go home for the day; or can stay at your center. This is an effective policy because the same injury may be considered to be an emergency that requires medical treatment by the parent of one child and a non-issue for another parent. Parents are very different in their interpretations of minor injuries. You can't go wrong when you lay out the details and let the parent make the call; however, you definitely can be wrong and have further ramifications if you make a judgment call and the parent disagrees.

Make sure the parents understand that you must be able to contact them at any time. Emergencies are just that; they aren't planned and will not come at a convenient time when a parent is readily available. In addition to having a good emergency phone number for the parents, it is important that you also have additional contact information for close relatives such as grandparents who could come and take care of the child if needed.

Most parents are very responsive and will drop everything to get to their child. Sometimes you will find other responses which include being angry at having to leave work; blaming the center for the accident; and even having a fear of taking a child to the emergency room because they are afraid it will lead to a CPS investigation for the injury. This is particularly true of parents with "accident prone" children who have to make a number of trips to the emergency room or doctor's office due to injuries. Some children are just more likely to have accidents and injuries. This can be due to the child having less coordination skills, being more rambunctious, or other reasons.

The emergency policies paperwork, must also state that your center and staff have the right to make decisions on behalf of the child if the parent or appropriate emergency contacts are not available. This is essential because even after all of the policies are put in place, it is possible for a child to have a medical emergency while in your care, and you are not able to reach the parent. In that case, the manager or someone in a lead position at the center must take on that custodial role. This extends beyond calling 911 and obtaining emergency services. This means that the designated staff member must get the child's emergency care permission slip; travel and stay with the child; and make appropriate decisions on the child's behalf until the parent can be there.

A final form of emergency that must be considered is that of a total center evacuation. For safety purposes, you must have a plan for evacuating the entire center. An example of needing to evacuate the entire building would be a gas leak. Determine a place that could sufficiently handle all the children and staff from your center. Examples of an appropriate evacuation center would be: a library, senior center, or school. The location and procedures should be included in policies that are provided to parents. Determine how you would relocate all the children to alternate location and how you will contact parents. Thankfully, the chance that you will ever have to implement this scenario is very slight; however, during an emergency is not the time to decide how it should be handled.

Responsibility Extends Past Your Center

Your responsibility for the health and well being of the children in your care extends far past the doors of your building and the boundaries of your property. You and your staff are caregivers and providers for the children in your care. If you suspect a child is being abused or neglected it is not only your responsibility, but also your legal obligation to report this to the state's child welfare agency for investigation.

Remember the importance of documentation; write everything down. Make it easy. One method is to provide a notepad or spiral notebook for each teacher. This provides a means for keeping track of any concerns. Be sure to have the staff member who is documenting include the date; straightforward information of facts; and leave out any non-factual information such as feelings. The majority of documented things will not have any long term significance. However, if you document each thing and you see a trend or something significant, this will be the information that you will need to provide.

6

Children's Health

In this chapter, you will discover how to create policies and procedures for maintaining the health of the children including:

- Overview of Keeping Children Healthy
- Health Regulations
- Health Policies
- Health Practices
- Minor Allergic Reactions
- Severe Allergic Reactions
- Food Allergies
- Pet Allergies
- Everyday Illnesses
- Major Illnesses
- Chronic Illnesses

Overview of Keeping Children Healthy

Keeping children healthy in a group environment can be challenging. In a childcare environment with many children indoors in classrooms together, germs are easily shared. Health regulations, policies, care of the environment, and managing illnesses are the keys to keeping children healthy and minimizing the spread of disease.

Health Regulations

Integrating all of the regulations, including health, into your centers programs can be time consuming. State health departments set out vaccination schedules to be completed by all children at specific ages along with other health related recommendations such as hearing and vision screenings. As a state licensed and regulated business, you will likely fall under these requirements to make sure these details are completed by the parents.

It is almost certain that children's vaccinations and required screenings will be part of your routine inspections. If the child's vaccinations or screenings are not complete, this will result in a violation for your center. Then you will still be required to enforce the regulations. This is done by requiring the parent to take the child to the doctor, complete the required updates, and provide the center with documentation. These forms then need to be submitted back to the state inspector to show that your center is in full compliance.

What about parents who do not believe in vaccinating their children or having hearing and vision screenings? For these parents, who are opposed to the standard vaccinations and screenings for personal, health, or religious reasons, there are options for documenting this. However, the states often do not lay these out easily. It may be necessary for you or the parent to find out what the state health department's requirements are and document accordingly. After appropriate documentation, this information can go into the child's file and will suffice as the center's compliance on the requirement for that particular child.

❖ Lesson From the Field: Parents Who Don't Believe in Vaccinations

One particular parent chose not to have his children immunized due to concerns over reactions and permanent damage that he believed was a real potential side effect of such vaccines. The details required to obtain a waiver of vaccinations and screenings were not clearly spelled out in the Texas childcare regulations. It only noted that it could be done. The parent went to the state health department and obtained the appropriate paperwork for our files to meet the criteria for his child's continued enrollment without the vaccinations routinely required by the state.

There are other issues which can arise with regard to completing required vaccinations. These can include such issues as: a shortage of a particular vaccine; a case where the insurance refuses to pay for the vaccinations until a particular date; or a doctor who refuses to perform hearing and vision screenings at the age that the state requires.

If there is a shortage of a particular vaccine, then document this within your files. Usually the child will have received all of the other vaccinations and will be missing only the one. If possible, have the child's doctor write down that there is a shortage of the vaccine. The doctor may also include a notation of when the vaccine is expected to be available. Put it in the child's file with the vaccination record. Always make it easy for the inspector. If she can't find or decipher the information, she will probably just say it's not there. In the case of a vaccine shortage, you may be able to find appropriate standardized documentation to simply attach to each impacted child's folder.

On situations where the insurance refuses to pay until a specified date, which may be exactly on the child's birthday or even later, the parent will most likely let you know that they are not going to have those scheduled vaccinations until the insurance will pay. You can get that information in writing. Will it stand up to an inspector? It depends on your inspector ... probably not.

In my experience, I did not find the inspectors were interested in any extenuating circumstances, only whether or not you met the rules at that point in time. There were occasions, although rare, where I just had to agree to go with it, even though philosophically I knew that I was justified in the way it was handled.

A third scenario is when the doctor refuses to offer the service at that age, or simply doesn't supply that service. It was quite surprising to find that some doctors did not perform routine health screenings recommended (and enforced for childcare attendance) by the state. In such situations, it may be necessary for you to help out the parents by providing information as to where they can have the service performed. It is a good idea to keep this kind of information. You are a resource for parents. Keep files of relevant resources available based on recommendations from other parents, information provided to the center, and government services which are available.

As stated, by including these vaccinations in your state regulations, the state is able to enforce their policies through childcare operations. How enforceable is it? Can you actually make a parent get their child vaccinated? Can you make a parent have the state recommended screenings? The answer is: only to a point. You can request that parents do this. It is advisable to make sure the parents understand that you are a licensed center and this is a state regulation. It is not a policy that you had a choice in developing. Based on this, in order to be enrolled in any licensed childcare center, these are required for the child.

What if they still won't have their child vaccinated, or provide you with the paperwork to opt out of the requirement? There are only two options left. The first option is: You can give them a deadline and let them know that they will not be allowed to return until the requirements have been met. The other option is: You can continue to allow them to be enrolled in your center and hope the file is not ever a part of an inspection. If it is inspected and you receive a violation, the only way to "correct" the violation will likely be to have the child dismissed from your center. (Please note that the second method would involve operating outside of the regulatory requirements and it is not recommended to do this under any circumstances.)

Health Policies

You must base your health policies on the health regulations required by the state; however, your own policies can be extended and more comprehensive than those regulations. You need to spell out specifically how you will handle certain events and how the health policies will be enforced for your center. These policies should be in writing and a part of your student handbook. In addition, you may want to update the information and reinforce particular parts that seem to create issues as needed, by providing parents with notes and reminders of those policies. Having stated health policies are essential, but just as in other areas, it doesn't mean the parents actually read them.

Enrollment forms should include a place for parents to list allergic reactions and the appropriate solution if those reactions are severe (such as the need for an epinephrine auto-injector like the EpiPen). Allergic reactions can range from mild to life threatening. If the reaction is severe and requires medicine in the event of contact with the allergen, then make sure the parents provide the center with that required medication. You must keep the medicine available along with documented permission to use the medicine if needed. It is best to keep the permission to use the medicine at the front of the child's file so that it is easily accessible in the case of emergency. It should include medication instructions and appropriate dosage amounts noted by a doctor.

One of the most significant health policies is that of how to handle allergies. This is a particular concern in the areas where allergic reactions can cause life threatening situations for children. It can also be a very complex situation to manage due to the fact that the more children there are in your care, the more allergies you will have to manage.

Some allergies you may experience in your center include:

- ✓ Allergies to specific foods
- ✓ Allergies to food additives
- ✓ Allergies to baby wipes
- ✓ Allergies to topical products (such as powders and creams)
- ✓ Allergies to medicines (very important in case of emergencies)
- ✓ Allergies to dust
- ✓ Allergies to latex (found often in bandages and gloves used for diapering)
- ✓ Allergies to animals
- ✓ Seasonal allergies

The list can go on and on. One effective means for managing the different children's allergies and health needs is to post them or keep them with the daily attendance sheets that stay with the class at all times. However you choose to manage the information, these lists should be readily available for the staff members on duty including those who prepare food.

Health Practices

Be aware of what creates a biohazard. Bodily fluids such as blood, vomit, and fecal matter should be handled carefully. These things should be handled by staff wearing gloves. I also recommended that materials soaked with potentially hazardous bodily fluids either be sent home for the children's parents to handle or thrown away.

❖ Lesson From the Field: Safety and Bodily Fluids

The health and safety of both my staff and my children were of the greatest importance to me. This stood out in my decision of how to handle bodily fluids which may be hazardous. I stood firm on my choice to not wash any materials that had blood, vomit, or feces on them in our center's washing machine. Parents do not always appreciate this choice when their favorite outfit is now stained from having blood on it all day and they believe that the staff should have washed it for them. Each time I had an angry parent, I would explain it this way.

"I do it for the health of all the children." The parent should understand the value of this in the long run, as I always made sure that children never came into contact with clothes or towels that had been used to clean up bodily fluids.

Diarrhea and potty training can put this methodology to the test, as some parents were not happy that the child's clothes still had some fecal matter on them when they get home. My staff dumped the obvious feces in the toilet and the soiled clothes were sent home in a disposable plastic bag. It is then the parent's choice if they want to put it in their washing machine or throw it away.

Choose how you want to handle such health issues and then stick to it. Be consistent and explain the health value of your choices for all of the children including their own child. Don't make apologies. Your responsibility is to make decisions which promote the best health of all the children.

Minor Allergic Reactions

Allergies can be mild such as seasonal allergies; reactions to poison ivy; and extra swelling caused by a mosquito bite. Some parents will overreact to some of the smallest allergic reactions. It is actually quite common for some parents to become very angry when a child comes home with a couple of mosquito bites!

As a general matter of policy, it is best whenever possible, to have parents apply any sunscreen or bug spray prior to children coming to the center. It lessens the chance that you will apply a product which may cause an allergic reaction in a child. You also want to get permission to apply such topical products in situations where it is necessary. When you apply these products, use them sparingly and only with express written permission.

❖ Lesson From the Field: Is It An Allergic Reaction?

Benjamin's mom brought him to me to show me his rash. I looked and wasn't really concerned. I asked the obvious questions to determine if it was allergy related. Had they changed laundry detergent or eaten something different? I said I would keep an eye on it. Only a short time later, his teacher made the observation that two other children had very pink little cheeks like they were too warm. Then we determined it was fifths disease. We had multiple cases and had not noticed. It was not an illness that required exclusion according to regulations. It just ran its course like a mild cold.

One additional note on minor childhood diseases: Some minor children's illnesses, such as fifths disease, have the possibility of being harmful to an unborn child. Remember to take care of your staff and pay attention to any special needs they may have as well.

Severe Allergic Reactions

More significant reactions include things such as allergic reactions to bee stings, latex allergies, and food allergies. A child with allergies isn't really hard to manage for the most part; however, when you have many children with many different allergies, it can become really difficult to make sure each child avoids contact with a trigger for his allergic reaction. Children who have the potential to have a severe or life threatening allergic reaction may require one step further, an epinephrine auto-injector or other emergency medication to be kept at the center in case of an emergency. If you have a child with such severe allergies make sure that you have the appropriate emergency supplies on hand along with written permission to administer them. The staff must also be trained in how to use the emergency supplies if needed.

- ❖ Lesson From the Field: Keeping Emergency Medicine Current

    At my center, we had a child who had a severe allergy to nuts. The parents had required an EpiPen in case of emergency. The EpiPen expired and after several reminders, the parents still had not brought a replacement. At that time it was necessary to provide a deadline in writing that stated the parents were either to provide a new EpiPen or sign a written form stating that it was no longer necessary. This was necessary to provide for the child appropriately as well as to manage the potential liability for the center should the child have an allergic reaction.

Food Allergies

Food allergies are one of the most prominent allergies. A reaction to nuts is a common food allergy. For this reason many centers choose to go "nut free." This can be important as a severe reaction to something, such as peanuts, can include just being near peanuts or peanut butter without ever ingesting the food. There are a number of other nuts that also may create an allergic reaction in children. In cases such as this where many children have a reaction and it doesn't have to be a prominent part of the center's food service; it's easier to just make sure it isn't ever served. In addition, many children's food projects include peanut butter. You will have to substitute something else or use projects which do not include peanut butter.

Going nut free also includes letting the parents know. One of the most popular children's sandwiches is still peanut butter. All of the parents have to understand not to bring peanuts or peanut products into your center. This extends to party food that parents may bring in as well. If a parent brings in peanut butter, you should not serve it. Explain to the parent why, so it doesn't happen again and send it back home. If that happened to be the child's lunch, then you will have to provide a different food to replace it. Even when one of the parents makes a mistake or violates a policy, your responsibility is to take care of the child.

With regard to other food allergies and food service, you have the option of posting and keeping up with all the food allergies; or removing particular foods from the menu if they are not something that you feel is necessary to serve. Common examples of other food allergies include milk products, eggs, wheat, and processed meats. If you do serve foods that children in your center are allergic to, then you have to create a system to insure the children with the allergy are not served that food. The choice of how to handle it can be based on the size of your center, the number of children with food allergies, and the specific foods. Make your policies based on what is easiest, most accurate, and best meets the needs of all the children in your center. Food allergies are discussed further in Chapter 10: Food Service.

Pet Allergies

If you choose to have pets in the center, even little animals such as hamsters, it is necessary to put it in your registration paperwork and policies in order to have written notice provided to parents. In addition, if you add a pet, you should only do so knowing that none of the current children in care have allergies to this particular pet. It is also necessary to monitor any animals around the building, even those brought in by well meaning family members. They are often very proud of their new puppy or kitty and want to bring it to show their friends. On multiple occasions, I had family members walk in to pick up their child with an adorable new puppy in their hands to show everyone. It seems harmless enough but at the time I had children with severe allergies to pet dander.

Everyday Illnesses

Refer to your state regulations for information on childhood illnesses, these documents should provide information on when a child must be excluded from care, when he may return, and which illnesses must be reported to your local health agency. Following allergies, one of the most common health issues you will deal with on a regular basis are colds, viruses, and other minor illnesses. You must have a policy in place as to what illness conditions you will allow in your center and when it is necessary for a child to be excluded from your center. The policy must include the state requirements; however, you have the option to provide even stricter standards if you feel it is needed. The fact that it is a group environment filled with small children who freely spread their sweet hugs and kisses along with their germs to others, means that it is highly subject to contagious diseases. It is important to sanitize regularly and thoroughly. Teach children good health and hygiene habits. Insure that the center is as clean and healthy as possible. Even when working diligently to prevent it, at times illness outbreaks will still happen.

Remove ill children from the others as soon as you notice they are sick. The sick child can sit in the office with an administrator or secretary if possible. Try to minimize any exposure of illness to the other children in the classroom. With respect to illnesses involving fever, specify in your health policies at what temperature point a parent will be required to pick up the child.

If you send a child home ill, be sure to specifically relay to the parent when he is allowed to return. Remind the parent of your policy: "Remember our policy is that if a child vomits at school, he must go home. Jason must be free of fever and have not vomited or had diarrhea for

24 hours before he can return to the center." If you don't do this, often you will see the child back the next morning even though he is still sick.

What do you do when a child arrives ill? Often this is not caught until the child has already been dropped off. If you do recognize that the child doesn't look well, grab that thermometer while the parent is standing there and check for a fever. If the child has a fever, send the child home with the parent in order to avoid exposing the rest of the children in care. This is difficult to do as the parent is already on their way to work and clearly didn't plan to stay home for the day; however, you are following your own established guidelines and protecting the health of all who are in your care.

What if the child appears ill but only has a low grade fever when you check? He hasn't met the absolute requirement by policy that requires exclusion from care. In this situation, you can let the parent know that you will continue to monitor the child's fever and overall well being; if it gets any worse you will call. This lets the parent know that there is a pretty good chance he will have to leave work so he can prepare for that possibility. Likewise, if a child who is already in care begins to feel poorly, you can give the parent a phone call at work to let him know that you are watching this to see if it gets worse. Tell the parent that if the child does get worse, you will be giving him another phone call and he will have to come take the child home. It helps the parent to prepare in case that happens. Some parents are very diligent and will say they are coming anyway to pick up the child so they can take her to the doctor or home to rest.

❖ Lesson From the Field: When Complaints Don't Make Sense

Miles came in with his father, who stated that the child was having an allergic reaction to mosquito bites that he had gotten when he stayed all day last week. The teacher that was outside on the day in question said he didn't look like that the last day he was at school. His little face was covered in very red infected looking dots. We looked into the details and clarified our information. Then I called the mother and spent 45 minutes on the phone while she insisted it happened at school.

I wanted to rule out chicken pox which appear quickly and can look like mosquito bites. Miles also had bites on his legs which appeared infected and a big scrape on his arm which was covered. He constantly picked at all of these scabs. His mother stated that in the evening when she had pulled the bandages off of his legs, the sores looked really bad. She described them as green, crusted, and oozing. She took him to the doctor and he was diagnosed with impetigo which is contagious. The red spots all over his face were due to the internal infection which probably began with the elbow scrape that had been picked at constantly. He was out for almost a week until all of the sores healed.

Major Illnesses

The third level of illness includes sicknesses that happen much less often and are more severe. These can be contagious diseases such as chicken pox and the flu. The policies and procedures are the same, but the spread of such illnesses can be even more problematic. Prevent the spread of such diseases in the same way as everyday illnesses, by sanitizing diligently.

Refer to your state's requirements for reporting diseases. The incident of certain diseases can require the center to report the illness cases to the health department. Usually this is just for documentation of disease outbreaks in the geographical area; however, in extreme situations, the health department can temporarily close a center to stop the spread of an illness.

If an illness is spreading through the center, whether it is a stomach virus or the flu, make sure parents know. Send notes home explaining the illness and advising parents to keep their children at home if they exhibit any of the symptoms. If they are in doubt, advise them to call you to discuss their child's condition, before they come to the center. Communicate the importance of parent cooperation in keeping sick children at home so that the illness will not spread. In addition, be extra diligent in sending children home at the first sign of illness to stop the spread of disease.

On the occasions where the stomach virus seems to be rampantly spreading through the center, take additional precautions. This often means late nights staying at the center sanitizing all of the materials and areas. These illnesses can be very challenging as they are highly contagious and spread through the center impacting both children and teachers alike. These outbreaks can be some of the most frustrating times as you deal with: multiple children vomiting or having diarrhea during the day; cleaning and sanitizing; separating children; calling parents; working short-staffed due to ill teachers; and staying late to do deep cleaning of the children's toys, activities, and environment.

In rare cases, media publicity and the fear of the unknown can take on a scare of its own. When the concern is raised regarding a particular illness, you will see extreme reactions in some parents. When swine flu was first brought to everyone's attention, it was not known how extreme the illness would be. The media created a great focus around it and emphasized the fear of a great pandemic. It created extreme situations of fear such as the following example:

❖ Lesson From the Field: Health Policies

One particular year, there was a great media attention and related fear of H1N1 or "swine flu." It was highly publicized and there was fear of a wide spread pandemic. We had a little boy who was sent home ill one day. His mother called back later and said that he had been diagnosed with the swine flu. Because it was an illness of concern at that time, it was necessary to communicate with parents in a note that a child in care had been diagnosed with it and they should watch for symptoms. In addition, if their child exhibited such symptoms, they should keep him home in order to keep it from spreading (just as with any other virus that can spread quickly in an early childhood center). We had a couple of inquiries but that was all, with the exception of one parent who was extremely disturbed by the potential exposure to the swine flu.

This parent was very disturbed and overreacted dramatically, stating that she didn't want her daughter to get it and that she did not want to get the swine flu. (I chose not to respond with the obvious ... that none of us wanted to become ill.) Her anger went even further, when I would not verify if the child was in her child's classroom for confidentiality purposes. It was important to inform parents of the health issues. It was just as important to protect the identity of the child who was ill. It was not his fault or his family's fault that he became ill.

In summary, the child who had the flu had only attended for two days and the parents found it necessary to withdraw him from the program for personal reasons. I was in touch with the mother later; and she relayed that further diagnoses indicated he hadn't had the swine flu after all; it was the regular flu strain.

The dreaded case or cases of head lice is another common health issue in childcare centers. Even if you have never had a case, don't be too confident. It probably will happen at some point. It is easily spread in environments where children are close together. Head lice can be spread from close contact with a child who has an active case of lice; children sharing hair brushes or hair accessories; children's jackets which are hung close and touching each other; blankets and bedding children use; and soft spaces within the center such as pillows in a reading center.

Watch for children who are dramatically scratching their heads. Head lice are extremely itchy and irritating when there is a full blown outbreak on a child's scalp. It can be very difficult to spot if you don't know what you are looking for. On one occasion, I had a parent let me know that the child only had a rash because it had already been checked by a doctor. We determined he had head lice. It had been diagnosed as a rash by the doctor. If you suspect a child has head lice, then it is necessary to look through the hair all the way to the base of the scalp.

If it is determined that the child does have head lice, the best solution is to send the child home along with all of her belongings. Provide detailed instructions in how to handle removing the lice (and nits) from the child's hair; all of her "soft" personal items (jacket, blanket, pillow, etc.); and in her home environment. In addition, you must now treat the affected areas at the center including: washing and cleaning all soft items; notifying parents of a case of head lice and what to watch for; sending home all of the children's blankets and jackets to be washed; and sanitizing the areas used for the storage of children's bedding. Diligently monitor the center for any more signs of children with lice. It is possible to prevent the spread of lice and any major outbreaks. As always, attacking the problem quickly and effectively is the best method.

Chronic Illnesses

❖ Lesson From the Field: Chronic Illness and Group Environment

Levi's was an absolutely adorable little boy with some ongoing minor health concerns. His dad dropped him off in the morning and asked that his outdoor activity be limited. He went outside in the afternoon while only one teacher stayed inside to clean and sanitize. Sanitizing was done daily when the children were outside so they were not exposed to the cleaners. His mother came in very upset that he had been outside even a little while. She said "his little lungs couldn't handle it" and he was not supposed to be outside at all. Of course the reality is that we didn't always have someone to stay in with only one child. When children are too sick to be outside and do other normal daily preschool activities, then they are too sick to be at school.

The problem becomes when parents want "babysitter" type care in a group environment. Often this happens when a child has a runny nose or something minor. The parent wants the child to stay indoors all day. Large centers that rotate outdoor time may be able to accommodate such requests. In smaller centers, it can be more difficult. In small centers, when the teachers and their classes go outside, the only options are for a child to sit in the office (usually reserved for punishments) or sit with the teacher who is cleaning up and preparing activities indoors. Later in the afternoon, often all of the teachers may be outside. This does not leave an extra person to sit inside the building with one child.

Be very diligent in your efforts toward cleanliness and health. These are very important and are a huge responsibility. Your efforts will receive a nice payoff as fewer children and teachers are sick and good health is maintained for everyone involved in your center.

7

Supervision of Young Children

In this chapter, you will examine the areas of supervision when working with infants through preschool age children including:

- Supervision Overview
- Building Design
- Methodology, Supervision, and Classroom Management
- Schedules and Attendance
- Discipline in Early Childhood Programs
- Spills and Accidents
- Naptime

Supervision Overview

The supervision of very young children is an enormous and vitally important responsibility. There are many elements to the supervision and safety in programs for infants, toddlers, and preschool age children. Building design, classroom layout, methodology, schedules, attendance records, discipline, classroom management, and naptime procedures are all components of a quality childcare program.

Building Design

The design of the building can have a large impact on the supervision of children. A building that was originally designed and constructed to be a childcare center will provide a layout that is easier to supervise. Many centers are in buildings which were not originally built for children's programs. These buildings can create really nice spaces for children's programs; however, they will usually incorporate a few more logistical challenges.

❖ Lesson From the Field: Building Design and Supervision

The center that I owned was a renovated old fashioned house. I loved the house and how it provided a wonderful foundation for the specific type of program I had designed. It was decorated in bright pastel colors and it provided a lovely "homey" feel and experience for children. However, the fact that it wasn't designed specifically for childcare, required additional diligence in supervising areas. An example was that the front door led directly into a classroom instead of a reception area. In addition, when a class went outside it meant walking through another classroom. There were not large hallways that are typical of buildings built specifically for childcare centers.

If your center doesn't have a designated reception area and has doors that lead directly from classrooms to the outdoors, make sure that you have an experienced teacher in such rooms who is able to carefully supervise exits. This is to monitor children, as well as adults coming in and out of the building.

Methodology, Supervision, and Classroom Management

The methodology and curriculum design of your center will create elements that impact your supervision. If you utilize a traditional childcare environment where children are free to play most of the day, then supervision can be more relaxed. If however, your design is based on a structured classroom model, then there will be a stricter level of supervision and discipline.

In any classroom management setting, the active supervision of children is paramount. Teachers must be trained and the concepts of active supervision stressed. Caregivers must be engaged in supervision at all times when they are on duty. This means that they must not be using cell phones for talking or texting; chatting with other teachers; or leaving the classroom unattended. Yes, there are teachers who will walk out of a classroom and leave the children unattended either on purpose for "just a minute" or because they are just not paying attention. It is hard to imagine, but there are centers in which leaving a classroom unattended for a short period is routine and accepted; never let this happen in your center. It clearly doesn't constitute a well managed quality center. Active and consistent supervision is critical to insure a safe environment. Teachers must also be careful and be aware of potential hazards. Many accidents can be prevented by good teachers with active supervision.

Schedules and Attendance

Children should be allowed to do a number of different things throughout the day to keep their day interesting. Provide them with multiple types of experiences and creative learning opportunities. This includes opportunities for lessons, indoor free play, art projects, active outdoor play, and rest time.

Staff members should always know how many children are in their classroom and they should have a written or printed list of children with them at all times. This list remains with the class when students are changing rooms, going outside, and even going into the dining area. Children should be signed in when entering and signed out each day when leaving. Keeping up with the children in care is not as simplistic as it sounds. Documenting and keeping the paperwork with the teachers and children is important.

Make sure that all children are accounted for at all times. This includes checking before and after changing rooms, going outside, returning into the building, and other such changes. Children can get lost simply moving between rooms if the teacher doesn't pay attention. There are many examples of why this is important. Here is one example:

❖ Lesson From the Field: Importance of Sign-In and Sign-Out Records

> *While the morning teacher was on duty, a preschool age boy's father picked him up early for a special activity together. The child was not signed out by the father or by the teacher on duty. When the afternoon teacher came in and took over she was missing a child! This was a scary moment for the teacher and the management. Documenting every child's entry and exit, along with knowing where every child is at all times, is critical.*

Discipline in Early Childhood Programs

Learning how to behave appropriately is part of a young child's education. There will be temper tantrums, yelling, hitting, and crying moments. Teach children how to behave. Provide examples and explain situations. Stress to children the importance of "using their words" rather than pushing or hitting. For the most part, this is just a part of young children learning how to solve problems in their world. Re-direction and discipline measures such as sitting out of an activity for a few minutes are appropriate means for correcting these behaviors.

You will also encounter chronic and more extreme behaviors. These are not near as prevalent and only a small percentage of children will exhibit such behaviors. These extreme behaviors can be very difficult to manage. Such behaviors can include very violent outbursts when angry children will hit or attempt to injure other children or staff members. A child in a violent rage should be removed from the classroom so that she will not hurt others. Some children can be very strong when they are in the middle of such an episode, and can even be challenging for an adult to manage.

As a director, you are responsible for the safety of all the children. It is good to attempt to work on behaviors when possible; however, there will be times when it is beyond what you are able to manage. You are not the parent and your disciplinary options are very limited. If you cannot control a child's extreme behavior with appropriate methods such as removing him from the classroom; sitting him out of an activity; or missing recess; the parent should be called to pick up the child.

Every time there is an incident, make a written report for the parent and keep a copy in the child's confidential file. When the parent continually gets these reports, she will understand the significance of the situation. The parent should be working with you to correct the behaviors. If the parent won't work with you, or if you are unable to correct the child's violent behaviors and it continues even with the parent's efforts, you must take further action. It will most likely be necessary to let the parent know that you are no longer able to keep the child at your center. Extreme children's behaviors are discussed in details in Chapter 16: Children's Behaviors.

Spills and Accidents

All children should bring a backpack to preschool with a change of clothes every day. Accidents will happen. These are often toileting accidents but such occurrences also include spills, vomit, and blood, as well as friends spilling or vomiting on another child! It is not unusual when accidents occur for a child to not have a change of clothes … even when it is your policy.

Now what do you do? Keep a stash of "extra clothes." These can be lost and found clothes that never went home, or donated clothing from parents and staff. They often don't fit well, but it's better than having a child stay in soiled clothing while you wait on a parent to arrive with more. It also saves the parent having to take off work to deliver the clothes. One other suggestion is to keep extra pull ups, in several sizes, to put on children when they don't have a change of underwear.

Naptime

Naptime can be a challenging time as your staff works to get all of the mats or cots laid out for the children; all of their bedding on their mats; all of the children to their mats; and finally all of the children quiet and sleeping. Naptime requires a plan for consistency using the same routine day after day. Provide a calm and quiet atmosphere so that all of the children can rest. Teachers should be patient, firm, and consistent. They should be down on the floor or at the mats, covering children, patting backs, and helping them fall asleep. The more consistent the process, the smoother it will run, and the faster children will get to sleep.

It is best to place each child's mat or cot in the same place each day. Also, allowing children to bring something, that makes them feel comfortable to sleep with, is a good way to create a positive naptime experience. Items from home such as a stuffed animal or a special pillow help make children relax and feel good at naptime. (Remember to be careful of items which are not appropriate sleeping materials for children under age two.) Soft background music can contribute to a comfortable atmosphere. Teachers need to be firm, yet patient and supportive as they pat backs, speak softly, and help the children be still and rest. There should be a plan of an alternate activity for children who have rested for a little while but did not fall asleep. These children need something else to do for the remainder of the nap time. Looking at books or another quiet activity done at their mat or cot is a good plan for these children.

Supervision of Young Children

Supervision is a greatly encompassing subject which falls into a number of categories. Additional information on supervision related to specific topics is found in the following chapters: supervision of outdoor playtime is covered fully in chapter 8; supervision as it relates to children's safety is discussed further in chapter 5; and supervision of meals is covered in detail in chapter 10.

8

Outdoor Supervision

In this chapter, you will explore the concepts and policies inherent in providing good outdoor supervision including:

- Outdoor Supervision Overview
- Staffing for Outdoor Supervision
- Managing Changing Numbers
- Active Supervision
- Playground Fill Material
- Playground Equipment

Outdoor Supervision Overview

Supervision of outdoor activities such as free play time on the playground is absolutely critical for safety and accident prevention. Even in very structured environments, this is when children are able to run, play, and be very active. It is a wonderful time of day that allows children much needed exercise, free play, and social time; however, it is also the time where children are more likely to sustain injuries due to the increased level of activity.

Staffing for Outdoor Supervision

There should always be at least two teachers on the playground. This allows for one to take children in for the inevitable trips to the "potty." In addition, if a child is hurt or needs additional care, one teacher is able to go with the child while the other can remain outdoors with the other children. Children can never be left alone … not even for a moment. Make sure that the teachers are well aware of this and have been provided appropriate staffing to handle such needs.

Having several teachers on the playground should provide good supervision, but it isn't always the case. In order to fully utilize multiple teachers on the playground, the teachers must stay spread out over the area of the playground so that all areas can be supervised. Teachers must remain standing up. Chairs should not be provided for teachers on the playground. Teachers are not on a break while supervising the playground. Just the opposite, teachers must be walking around the playground, actively supervising, and definitely not sitting down or standing in groups chatting.

Gates and fences should be actively supervised as well. There may be times when children try to open and run out of gates, climb over fences, or find a hole to crawl under. These are all fun games for small children, but serious safety issues for teachers to monitor.

❖ Lesson From the Field: Children Trying to "Escape" the Playground

The children said they were trying to "escape" as they attempted to open a gate which had a pole secured into the ground. Four children had worked together and the teachers saw them as they managed to get the gate opened. They were stopped and notes went home to parents. If they did it again the parents would be called to come and get them. This was due to safety ramifications including the possibility of letting smaller children out.

Children shouldn't be allowed to lie down on the playground. It is a safety hazard. They may be run over by other children who don't even notice them on the ground. In addition, be aware of excess heat. Watch for overheating and monitor the daily temperature, humidity, and ozone reports to determine when it is not appropriate to be outdoors. Allow children frequent water breaks and keep them hydrated.

Managing Changing Numbers

A list of all of the children (usually one per class) must accompany the group everywhere they go. This is the official roster and it should accurately reflect the children within that class throughout the day. Children should be signed in and signed out on this form. That way there is always an accurate account of who is in care, even when children arrive late or leave early.

These details can make what seems very simple: "How many children are in the group?" actually a complex and ever changing component. An example would be: five children went inside to go potty; two went home with their mother; and one was sick and went to sit in the office and wait for a parent. The number of children should accurately reflect how many are on the playground. This number has to be constantly updated because in just a few more minutes: the 5 children who went in are back outside; 3 more went in to go potty; one more went home for the day; and another class joined the group on the playground. All the teachers on duty should be aware of how many children are on the playground and make adjustment every time there is a change.

All children should be accounted for when going outside to play and when returning into the building. This should mean an actual check off of each child … not a head count. When a great deal of change is happening, particularly near closing time, this is very important. The children are often playing outside and must return indoors. Each child must be checked off the list while lining up to go inside and again once inside. In addition, each time a group leaves the playground, an administrator should go and check the entire playground to make sure there are no children left behind.

Active Supervision

Carefully check the roll sheets and monitor all children when going outdoors and returning back into the building. Leaving a child outdoors is something that happens from time to time at centers … and it shouldn't ever happen! Numerous centers have had this event happen, and it usually happens under the same circumstances. The number of children the teachers thought they had was incorrect. The reality is that childcare is a hectic world and what is really a small mistake of miscalculating by one child, can end up with a significant consequence of a child being left alone. Most citations of this event, document that the teachers counted children and thought they had the right number. As discussed, particularly during outdoor times, it is easy to make a mistake on the number of children being supervised. It is imperative to have a system which provides a back-up procedure to protect against this mistake. The system of just keeping up with the numbers can fail.

Children will "hide" or simply be too busy playing to notice. It can happen and numbers that change often can be wrong. Individually check off every child on the list and have a supervisor walk the entire playground after each time children return indoors. This provides not only a first check but also a double check. Build in practices which ensure safety through procedures. Be safe and be careful. Prevent incidents that may put children at risk and create detrimental occurrences for the business by placing the center under investigation by the state for lack supervision. Consider including the following safety procedures in your daily operations.

Going to the playground and monitoring the playground procedures:

- ✓ Every child is signed in by verifying the accuracy of the roll sheet
- ✓ If a teachers signs a child in for a parent, she must include her initials
- ✓ A complete count must be done on leaving a room or exiting the building
- ✓ Another complete count must be done upon arriving at the new area
- ✓ Monitor playground numbers carefully
- ✓ Make sure every child that leaves is signed out and every child who is taken in for water, restroom, or first aid is accounted for

When returning the entire group inside:

- ✓ Children line up at the gate or door
- ✓ Check off every child by name

- ✓ After the class is back inside the building, have the teacher check off every child on the list (verifying not only numbers but individual children)
- ✓ After all of the children have gone inside, a supervisor walks the entire playground (taking care to look inside every climber and large toy on the playground)

Playground Fill Material

Playgrounds are usually required to have some form of fill material to soften a fall when there are toys which are higher off the ground. These materials are required to help protect children from falls, and yet many of these materials are made up of very small pieces … such as pea gravel. These small pieces, which are not allowed within a classroom, are widely available on the playground used by very small children. These fill materials do provide access to what is considered a choking hazard. Carefully supervise the very young children in these areas. Children choose to do some odd things at times. It is common for small children to attempt to eat the pebbles (or other fill material), or see if it fits in their nose or ears. They may also collect the items in their pockets and take them back into the classroom to play with later.

Playground Equipment

Choose your playground toys carefully. Commercial playground toys can be very expensive. These pieces of equipment generally do hold up well and will make a good investment over time. Most home playground equipment doesn't hold up well to the very active use of many children at a childcare center.

When you are first opening your center, it is often beneficial to choose smaller less expensive playground toys. Great choices for inexpensive outdoor toys are playhouses, sand boxes, and other stationary structures (such as pretend fire trucks and school busses) that will allow children to play in and on them. Blowing bubbles, outdoor chalk, outdoor paint, jump ropes, and lightweight balls are also good inexpensive choices for outdoor play. (One note, is that lightweight balls are lots of fun for children; however, be prepared to spend a great deal of time retrieving them from the other side of the fence as they seem to go over the top constantly.) These activities will give the children some fun outdoor play and yet will not cost large volumes of money. After becoming more established, you can slowly add one or two commercial pieces a year to your playground toys in order to build up your outdoor environment.

As you determine that you are ready to invest in commercial playground toys, choose carefully so that you make a good investment that will last for many years. As you choose larger and more expensive playground toys, pay careful attention to your state regulations and your insurance policy as well, regarding such play equipment. Certain types of toys will be outright banned while others will have additional regulations impacting their use. The height and movement of equipment will often dictate whether a use zone is required along with the size of the use zone if it is required. Acceptable fill materials and the depth required is also mandated within the state standards. When required, the addition of use zones, adds a great deal to the cost of the new outdoor play equipment. The selection of playground toys is discussed in detail in Chapter 5: Children's Safety.

Your playground is subject to inspection as part of your routine compliance inspections. Having playground equipment and toys which are banned by your state standards, will result in citations and the requirement to remove them. This creates not only regulatory issues but it also is a waste of money that could have been put to use in something with longer term benefits for the children.

Water activities are another consideration for summer programs. Look carefully at your state regulations and insurance coverage prior to scheduling water activities. State regulations in Texas have gotten much stricter on supervision requirements in recent years. In addition, while some insurance policies will cover water activities, others will not. Water activities can be as simplistic as sprinklers and wading pools or include water slides and even swimming pools.

Insurance plays a part in what is allowed in your program. Our insurance banned water slides several years into the program. We had to get rid of the purchased water slide that we had previously used each summer. As both state regulations and insurance restrictions became stricter, we found it necessary to eliminate our backyard water days in the summer in later years.

9

School-Age Programs

In this chapter, you will discover the various components of managing a successful school age program including:

- School-Age Overview
- School Year Programs
- Transportation Safety
- Full Day Programs
- Field Trips

School-Age Overview

School-age children are a very different group from younger children. They have different needs and the programs provided need to reflect those needs. Centers providing programs for older children need to make special accommodations for these children in programs, activities, and classrooms.

School Year Programs

During the school year, the school-age children are usually at school during the majority of the day. At this time, the primary needs for school-age children center on getting them safely transported to school in the morning then picking them up and returning them to the center. Depending on the meal policies, centers may offer breakfast before school. After school, the center is usually responsible for providing an afternoon snack, childcare, homework assistance, activities, and social time. Quality of care and programs are very important for school-age children. If you are offering programs for older children, it is important to place an emphasis on quality design of such a program.

Transportation Safety

One of the differences in the school-age program is the addition of transportation. This is usually when children are allowed to go on field trips in the summer and they are often taken to and from their schools each weekday. Transportation is a huge responsibility and it should be taken with a great degree of care and consideration for the safety of the school-age children. Appropriate and safe vehicles need to be utilized along with meeting all state regulations for safety seating. Check your local and state laws along with childcare regulations to make sure that your vehicles and safety seats meet all requirements for transporting children. Regular maintenance should be completed along with appropriate documentation of such maintenance on all vehicles used for transporting children. In addition, make sure the vehicle and liability insurance are appropriate for your needs and meet your state's childcare regulations. Be sure to keep a copy of the insurance policy inside the vehicle and update it each year as the policy renews.

Policies and procedures must be in place to make sure that children are safe while entering into vehicles, being transported, and being unloaded from those vehicles. Safety policies should include having only drivers with verified excellent driving records allowed to drive children. In addition, drivers should be carefully selected based on their attention to details to ensure that all safety procedures are followed. Drivers have a great deal of independence while they are out on the road with children; only your most reliable staff members should be allowed this position in order to ensure safety of the children. Copies of driver's licenses must be on file. Establish a calendar to make sure that drivers have their licenses renewed on time and are never driving with an expired license.

The management must make sure that the transportation vehicle and seating meet all legal and state regulation standards which can vary based on the type of vehicle as well as the age and size of individual children. In addition to safety procedures, centers that provide morning transportation to schools need to have specific policies in place for schedules. State a specific time those children must arrive by in order to eat breakfast before the transportation route begins. Also, make sure that the parents are aware of the daily departure time for the transportation. Parents must know what time the bus will leave. If they do not arrive by this time, the parents will be responsible for getting their own children to school that morning. This is an important policy because you cannot wait on parents who arrive late. It is not reasonable to make children late for school because one parent is late bringing their child to the center.

Daily procedures must be carefully adhered to for the safety of children being transported. The driver must carry a cell phone in order to contact the center or be contacted by the center if needed. In addition, a strict policy of not talking on that cell phone while in route must be in place. The telephone should only be used while the driver is pulled over and stopped at an appropriate place, and even then it should only be used to verify information regarding children. Typical things that may require a cell phone include: vehicle problems or other emergencies; children who are not at a school and are on the list to be picked up; and parents who call after the route began to say their child won't be picked up that day. There was an incident cited where a staff member from one center was clearly not responsible.

❖ Lesson From the Field: Care in Picking Up Children

This incident involved a driver of a childcare van who picked up an "extra child" and took him back to the ABC Childcare Center. The child went in and proceeded with the other children. Meanwhile, the parents, police, and school were trying to locate the missing child. My center was called, along with every other childcare center that picked up children from that particular school, to ask if we had brought back an extra child. The child was finally discovered at ABC Childcare Center by a parent picking up their own child. It was not until that time, that the staff at the center realized the child was not supposed to be there at all.

I did on one occasion have a little girl who was not enrolled at my center insist that she should get on my bus. Obviously, I didn't let her on the bus. Small children get confused or want to go home with a friend. It is up to the driver to make sure she is picking up the correct children. Drivers must have a list of all of the children and know the children. It is the staff member's responsibility to know who is to be on her bus and who is not. It is essential to verify that every child on the list is picked up or accounted for in another way. In addition, the staff member has the responsibility to see that there are no children on the bus that are not on the list of children to be picked up.

It is easy to see numerous safety concerns in the transportation of children simply by looking at the other vans and busses in the various school bus lanes. Just from looking at other childcare buses as you travel, you can observe that many centers have chaotic and unsafe transportation practices. This is often the case due to out of control children whose only supervisor is driving and not effectively able to manage the behaviors of the children on the bus. The reality is very few of these are actually cited as licensing violations; even though it is easy to see as you drive through school transportation lines. It is not easily viewed by licensing inspectors who inspect on site at the centers. As you evaluate your transportation procedures, consider the following bus safety concerns and safety practices that you may want to include.

Transportation Safety Violations to Consider:

- ✓ Children standing up and moving around
- ✓ Bus drivers that drive off before the children are even sitting down (much less buckled up safely)
- ✓ Children making inappropriate gestures out the windows
- ✓ Drivers who don't drive carefully and don't observe traffic rules

Transportation Safety Practices to Include in Your Policies:

- ✓ Verify that every child on the list has been picked up
- ✓ Make sure that all of the children are correctly and securely buckled into their seats
- ✓ Implement safe driving practices (including stopping at all railroad tracks, carefully observation of red lights, unprotected left hand turns, and other safe practices)
- ✓ Insure that drivers are careful when picking up, transporting, and dropping off children.
- ✓ Have drivers watch for inconsiderate people on the roads who do not have respect for the fact that children are being transported.
- ✓ Utilize maintenance procedures that insure the seatbelts are working properly and straps are not twisted.
- ✓ Require children to sit down, be buckled, and behave on busses.
- ✓ Do not allow toys, pencils, or other school work out due to safety concerns. (A fast stop could make a pencil or pair of scissors dangerous. In addition, scissors and pencils can be used to damage the bus or worse hurt another child.)

If you do encounter behavior problems on the route, the driver should find a place that is safe; pull off the road and stop; and then proceed to correct the children. Once the children have been corrected and it is safe to precede then the driver can continue. This is very important and at times necessary. One of the reasons that behaviors can be inappropriate on a bus is that the children believe there isn't anyone who has the ability to correct them. Once they understand that the driver is in charge, even though she is also driving, the behaviors should be much improved. If you continue to have problems with specific children, then the inappropriate behaviors should be addressed with documentation and parent notifications such as those discussed in Chapter 16: Children's Behaviors. If the behaviors continue to be disruptive then it may be necessary to remove the child from the program or deny transportation privileges to the child.

A list of all children being transported should be carried during transportation. The list should document: the arrival of children at the center; the school that they are transported to; and the time they are released into the care of the school after arriving at their destination. Children should only be allowed to enter the vehicle curbside. Do not allow children to cross in front of other vehicles or walk through the parking lot. The driver should take care to make sure each child is appropriately buckled into the vehicle. After transporting the children to the public school, the driver must make sure they exit the bus curbside; document the time they are released to the school; and make sure that they are accepted into the school by a staff member. The driver must watch until the children have completely entered the school building and are in the care of that school. Then the driver can continue to the next location to drop off other children.

After all of the children have been released into the care of their daytime schools, the driver will return to the childcare center. After parking the vehicle, the driver must look at each seat if it is a car or van, or walk the entire vehicle if it is a bus. This is to verify that there are no children on the bus. In addition, she will return to the building with the documentation list.

The list of children and documentation must remain at the center during the day. Parents must let the staff know if their child will not be riding home with you on a particular day. When parents call, it needs to be written down on the list immediately. The world of childcare can be very hectic with many phone calls, children's issues, and daily events. It's easy to forget something if it's not immediately documented. Take that few minutes to document that the child will not be picked up and include the initials or name of the person taking the message. That way, if there are any questions, they can be addressed to the person who took the message.

Afternoon pick up of children can have more difficulties than mornings. In the morning, the driver transports the children who have arrived and documents those that have not. In the afternoon, a number of things can happen. It is fairly common for a child to be missing from the bus line. At that point, the driver has to locate the child.

The public school teachers on duty can go back in and try to see if the child was checked out early by a parent. Also, the driver can contact the center so the director can begin calling the phone numbers on the child's file to locate the parent. The driver must wait until the child has been located before proceeding on the route. There are situations where the child is still at school and has been delayed. The policy should insure that the child is not left behind. Once the child has been located at the school; it has been confirmed that she has already been checked out; or it was determined that she was not at school that day; then the driver can proceed.

It is relatively common for a particular child to be the one that is not at the bus repeatedly. Certain parents will alter their schedules, by picking up their children often, and frequently forget to notify the center. It is a good policy to let parents know that it is always best to have the children use your transportation if possible. Exceptions to this include when the children are sick and miss school, or when they are taken home early. Parents who are able to pick up their children from school on certain days should be advised to simply meet the bus back at the center if possible.

Constantly switching the way a child travels home from bus to parent pick up can be very confusing on the child. If changes occur often, the child is more likely to get in the wrong group of children at school and therefore not be in line for your bus. This is a common problem for children who are picked up in different ways on different days. The more consistent your pick up route is, the more smoothly it will run. It creates a situation with fewer questions, problems, and mistakes if the children are all picked up on a routine basis and parents pick them up from the center.

❖ Lesson From the Field: When Picking Up Children Doesn't Go Smoothly

> *One child that I was supposed to pick up was not in the line to be picked up one afternoon. It wasn't that unusual but what followed certainly was. This particular school didn't provide good supervision for their childcare transportation students and there wasn't a teacher available to check on Lacy. I proceeded to the office accompanied by all of the other children on my route since I couldn't leave them unattended while I searched for the missing child. One of the children with me said she saw Lacy get into a car. I said that couldn't be right since she was*

supposed to be with us. (We had already called and verified with the parent that they had not picked up Lacy.)

We weren't able to find her through the school or communicating back and forth with the parents and staff at the center. After extensive efforts, we were finally able to validate that she did go home with a friend. This occurred after she was incorrectly told by a teacher that we had left her. Later the parent continued to accuse me of leaving without her even though we clearly had been at the school for the entire time until her location and her care was transferred back to her parent's responsibility.

After the children are returned to the center, they need to be unloaded curbside and greeted by staff already at the building. The driver needs to send the documentation sheet, of all children in care, into the building with the children. In addition, the staff members must count and verify that all of the children entered the building. Then make sure the caregiver inside the building knows how many children have come into the center. Does it seem like duplication? Yes, but remember there is no room for error. Children must be accounted for and kept safe at every step.

The final step entails that the driver park the bus and then (just as on the procedures for returning in the morning), she must walk the entire bus, or look in every seat for smaller vehicles. This step provides a double check to ensure that there are no children left in the vehicle. Children often fall asleep in the vehicles and if care is not taken to account for every child, sleeping children can be overlooked. Policies with multiple steps and some duplication may seem excessive but these are just the steps and double checks that will prevent mistakes that can be very serious. Over the years, there have been numerous citations of children being left in childcare vehicles. There are even instances where these mistakes have led to the death of a child. You can't be too careful!

Full Day Programs

School-age children will be at the center all day on many school holidays and during the summer. Programs should be planned for these children based on the needs and interests of school-age children. There are some times when the children really just want to play. Their days during the school year are filled with lessons, homework, and structure. Holidays during the middle of the school year are wonderful opportunities for older children to socialize and enjoy being a child. If there is only a day or two off from school, you may want to plan very little in the way of additional activities so that they can just enjoy free time, playing, and socializing.

When it comes to longer break periods, particularly summer break, there needs to be a program designed to keep the school-age children busy and entertained. A well planned summer schedule which includes arts and crafts, group activities, themed activities, special days dedicated to fun, along with free time for play and socializing really add to the impact and fun of a summer program. Depending on the mission of the center, educational activities to keep the children progressing academically over the summer are a nice addition to your summer program.

Field Trips

Providing field trips is a wonderful way to enhance the learning experiences and fun of summer programs for children; however, field trips are a huge responsibility when it comes to the safety of children. The actual locations to visit should be carefully selected, taking into account such things as: distance, heavy traffic, crowds, activities provided, and the safety of such activities. Remember to take into account how each particular location will impact the ability to keep track of every child ... including those that tend to be distracted and wander away. It is very common to see school-age children on childcare field trips that are all over buildings and almost totally unsupervised. This provides difficult situations for others and is very concerning from the standpoint of safety and supervision. This is another one of those situations that you won't find often in state violation records because it happens away from the center. It does happen frequently and it shouldn't. Great care and supervision should be a part of every field trip.

For your center, select the caregivers who will supervise the trip very carefully. Make sure there are enough caregivers to support the state requirements. In addition, consider the particular children's needs and the exact type of field trip. Some field trips may need more staff accompanying them than is required by regulations. Even if regulatory standards allow, there should never be less than two supervisors on a trip. This leaves one to supervise the children as they exit curbside and the other to go and park the bus. In addition, things like restroom stops; going back to the bus to get lunches; taking care of a child who becomes ill on the trip; and other such situations require more than one adult.

Ask for parent volunteers for field trips. Many parents enjoy joining you on field trips and provide additional supervision. Be sure to check your state standards and meet all requirements for parent volunteers. Also, be sure you know the parent volunteers well, and utilize good judgment when determining exactly what they will be responsible for on the field trips.

The same vehicle loading and unloading procedures used for transportation to and from school apply to field trips. In addition, it is advisable to have a center t-shirt that all children must wear on the field trips. Keep a few extra t-shirts to loan for the children who are supposed to go on the trip but forgot to wear their shirt on that day. The list of children on the trip should accompany the adult in charge at all times throughout the trip.

Just one child who has bad behavior can create quite a problem for the staff and group as a whole. Children understand when requirements are set forth for them and most will rise to the occasion. Set out guidelines for appropriate behavior for your program. Make a system, such as a weekly behavior chart and write down misbehaviors on the chart. When a child has too many misbehavior marks, then he is not allowed to participate in the field trip. Have another plan for those children who are not allowed to go on the trip. Typically such charts are for each individual trip; however, there are times when a child's behavior is so poor that it is important that he not be a part of any field trips. This information needs to be documented and shared with parents.

During the field trip, good student behavior is very important for the safety of all children. Go over behavior rules and requirements with the children before every field trip. Make sure they understand the rules. A simple reminder is usually all it will take for good behavior during the trip. There may still be instances when poor behavior has to be addressed during a field trip. If you allow children to go who have questionable behavior, including those that are distracted and may wander away, keep them very close and have them hold a caregivers hand.

Count, count, and count again! Field trips involve counting your children repeatedly throughout the entire trip. Constant monitoring of the children is absolutely necessary. A search of violations can reveal various accounts of children lost or left behind on field trips. The supervising staff must be extremely careful in every aspect of caring for children away from the center. Some younger children will tend to wander off when they see interesting things. Many of these younger children have only been on trips with their parents and have trouble remembering that it is a group activity and they must stay together.

Field trips are an immense responsibility and a great deal of work for staff members who supervise them. It is not a relaxing event. Most field trips go very smoothly because most children understand the need to behave well and that if they don't behave well, they will not get to go on future field trips.

10

Food Service

In this chapter, you will look into the options for food service and be able to evaluate which choices are best for your center including:

- Food Service Design
- Menus and Rotations
- Food Allergies and Religious Restrictions
- Children Who Bring Their Own Lunch
- Centers Which Do Not Provide Lunches
- No Outside Food Policies
- Purchasing Food
- Serving Food

Food Service Design

There are a number of ways to layout the food service for your childcare center. These begin with the most simplistic: where children bring their lunches, drinks, and snacks; and extend all the way to providing three meals, two snacks, and all of the drinks every day. Some centers even use the option of having meals catered and brought to the center by an outside company. This is an expense that would have to be passed on to the parents, but does eliminate the need for a commercial kitchen and the staffing of it. As a part of evaluating your food service options, make sure that you have talked with your local code representative and carefully scrutinized your state regulations. Utilize all of that knowledge as you evaluate your options.

When choosing which type of kitchen to use, a major consideration is how many children you will be feeding at each meal. Cost considerations should be evaluated as you determine what is best for you. If you are offering meals and snacks as a part of your program, then that cost has to be incorporated into your tuition.

Consider how far you will extend your food service. Lunches and snacks are the most common. Other considerations include: Will you serve breakfast to children in the morning? Will you serve dinner to children in the evenings? If you are offering a full food service program, it is very common to serve breakfast to children in the morning. The evening meal is less common; however, it is seen more in programs that are open later in the evening. It is also a big consideration for programs offering night care. If children are staying late in the evening or overnight then arrangements of some form must be made for those meals.

In the most basic set up, the food policy would consist of the children bringing their own lunches, drinks, and snacks for the day. The center can design policies as to how these will be stored. Also determine whether your staff will heat the lunches brought from home or whether those lunches must be "ready to eat." Other options can include things such as children bringing lunches while the center provides the snacks and drinks. Again, local codes vary but providing only snacks will usually not require an extensive kitchen set up.

Another idea to explore is the option of having a commercial kitchen in your center. It is a very nice amenity for parents and children but it can also be a very expensive undertaking for a center. Offering full meals means that you very well may have to meet all of the local code requirements of a restaurant. This area will typically fall under your local codes and the requirements can vary greatly. You can expect those codes to dictate many fine details including: equipment, food storage, sanitation methods, cooking procedures, cooking temperature requirements, hiring a certified food manager, and more. In addition, it is very predictable that those codes will change over time and require you to continue to spend money as you update your kitchen to meet newer codes throughout the years.

If you choose to cook meals, there are two basic types of set ups that you can choose from. One is a warming kitchen and the other is cooking "from scratch." Many childcare centers choose to use a warming kitchen concept. In this layout, the food is purchased already completely cooked and is stored as frozen or refrigerated products. These products are ready to heat through and serve. This is very efficient and many foods that children love to eat can be prepared this way. Purchasing frozen entrees and adding canned or frozen vegetables as side dishes can provide meals that children enjoy and these can be prepared with less time and effort.

Cooking from scratch involves the cooking of "raw food products" meaning meats and other foods have not yet been cooked. These products are purchased as fresh or frozen and then must be cooked through to recommended temperatures to ensure safety. It is another good option for producing good meals for children. This method will usually take more time in preparation and require the purchase of many separate ingredients.

Whichever type of food service you choose, select your children's meals and snacks wisely. Put consideration into offering foods that the children enjoy and that provide healthy balanced diets. Refer to your state regulations when choosing your menus. State regulations will often dictate exactly what foods and portion sizes are required. Offer different foods and find out what the children really enjoy. If some foods aren't eaten well after a few attempts, take them off the menu and try something else.

Another consideration when determining your menu is the age of children and avoiding foods or cuts of foods that pose choking hazards. This is a consideration for all small children; however, it is even more critical for very young children up through age two. Children up to two years old may not have all of their teeth in yet, which can make chewing up some foods properly more difficult. Research which foods pose choking hazards for young children and avoid those or when appropriate consider cutting them up into very small pieces. Make sure that your staff is trained to watch the children carefully while eating so that they are aware if any child has trouble with choking. All of your teachers should have training in first aid, including how to handle choking incidences in small children.

Evaluate all of your food service options including: having food catered to the center; having children bring their own food; providing a simple warming kitchen; and providing a full commercial kitchen with food made from scratch daily. If you have a small center and are feeding smaller numbers of children for meals, then having a warming kitchen can be less expensive. The food is likely to cost a little more because it is already prepared and just needs to be warmed up; however, the cost of having someone to prepare the food and buying all the many ingredients that it would take to cook from scratch is more expensive. In a smaller center with a warming kitchen concept, it is possible to have one or two of your staff members qualified to cook as a part of their daily duties. Then it isn't necessary to hire a separate person just to manage the kitchen.

If you are feeding a large number of children, then it may be best to cook from scratch. It creates a more complex food service process with longer hours dedicated to purchasing, storing, and cooking food; however, this may balance with the fact that it costs less per child. If you are cooking large volumes of food in a kitchen that relies on starting from scratch ingredients, it is likely that you will need to hire someone who is qualified to manage a commercial kitchen to do just that … cook and manage the kitchen.

The same considerations can go into the snack menu as well. Snacks can be as simple such as cutting up some seasonal fruit or serving cheese and crackers. Other snacks can require more preparation such as baking fresh muffins.

Drinks are another consideration in the food service. Drinking water should be considered carefully. If you are going to use tap water, then have it tested to make sure that it is safe. Other options include: companies which deliver large containers of bottled water or installing a filtered drinking water system. On a smaller scale, while you are just starting, it may be cost effective to have bottled water delivered to your center. Having bottled water delivered does mean having to: keep up with inventory; how much is needed; delivery schedules; along with storing and handling large bottles of water. Consider the cost of a water filtration system. Although expensive, this type of system can pay for itself in a very short period of time in a large center. Even in smaller centers, the cost of a filtration system will generally be less expensive in the long run.

Drinks offered with meals and snacks will generally include milk and juice. Make sure that your choices are healthy and good for the children in your care. Often children will eat at the center much more than they will eat at home. On a typical day, many children will eat breakfast, two snacks, and a lunch at the center and only dinner at home. For centers offering dinner, some children may be eating all of their meals at the center depending on how many hours they are in care.

Juice should be 100% fruit juice. It is common in some centers to substitute cheaper flavored punches or powdered drink mixes that are mostly sugar for the juice. As in all areas of childcare, the cost of providing for children must be balanced with the business bottom line. Do what is right for the children. Base your program's food service on high quality. Then make sure that your parents know what great things you are providing for their children. Many parents will pay more for those healthy quality meals. Remember to include information on the quality of your meals in your promotional paperwork and include the costs of providing good food into your tuition rates.

Menus and Rotations

Menus should be designed to create a rotation of foods for both variety and practicality. Well planned menus cut down on wasted spending on food and streamline purchasing for cost savings. An example would be serving the same vegetable on the menu twice in one week. In a smaller center, this can mean opening a very large can of vegetables and dividing it in half. You can prepare half of the can for one meal and refrigerate the other half for a meal later in the week. This is less expensive than opening several small cans and does not waste food.

Snacks can also be used in the rotation. Having various simple snacks throughout the week provides a great variety for children. At the end of the week you can include a "snack mix" or "trail mix" which can include leftover snack foods from earlier in the week.

Menus should rotate by the month. This allows you to streamline purchasing and predict how much of each item should be bought. It is a good idea to document how much is eaten at each meal and come up with appropriate amounts for purchasing on a regular basis. The food quantity purchased should allow: children to eat well; provide for refills; and allow for extra plates of food in case of spills. By paying attention to how much food should be allotted for each meal, you can significantly reduced wasted food and the costs associated with throwing out uneaten food.

Food Allergies and Religious Restrictions

There are a number of things which complicate the selection of food for the menu and the process of serving food. Many children have food allergies and shouldn't eat certain foods. This can be even more problematic if there are foods that children cannot even come into contact with. These are extreme allergies which some children have. An example would be children with an extreme allergy to peanuts. These children cannot even be in a room with peanuts much less eat them. This allergy extends to one of the favorite foods of many children … peanut butter. Peanut butter is very prevalent in children's lunches, and peanuts are very prevalent in other foods. Many snack foods (chips, crackers, and cookies) which do not actually contain peanuts are processed in plants that also process peanuts. These snack foods have the potential to be problematic for some children as well. In addition, many early childhood "cooking" projects include peanut butter as an ingredient. Many centers go "nut free" in order to keep children who are allergic, from coming into contact with this potentially hazardous food.

There are many other foods that will trigger allergic reactions in children. These can include allergies to wheat, milk, processed meats, certain vegetables, and even particular spices. How you will avoid exposing children to foods which create allergic reactions has to be a part of the center's policies. If it is a food that is not a regular or important part of your menu, you can consider eliminating the food from the menu. This works well in smaller centers. The larger the center and the greater the enrollment, the more this becomes a strategy that doesn't work well. In these cases, the center can continue to serve the food but has to find ways to make sure that the children with allergies do not receive the food.

An example of a food that some children can't have is milk. The center isn't going to stop serving milk. You must create procedures of how you will handle the situation and ensure the children who are lactose intolerant do not receive the milk served to most of the children. Parents can be required to bring a substitute drink, such as a container of lactose free milk for their own child to drink. The center will then be responsible for monitoring the expiration date and notifying the parents when more lactose free milk is needed.

When a main dish food is something that a child is not able to eat, then the center can either provide an alternative or require the child's parent to send a lunch from home on the days that food is served. Just be aware that many parents will not be diligent in keeping up with the menu and you still may find yourself needing to substitute some food for that child. The child is still in your care and still needs to eat a good lunch, even if the parent misses the details.

The same policies and procedures can be used when parents of children have religious preferences which do not allow particular foods. An example would be a Muslim family who does not eat pork. In this situation, you must decide if you will adjust for the child or require the parents to bring a separate lunch on these days. You must let the parent know which foods have pork. This often requires actually looking at the ingredient list on foods, particularly if your center uses a warming kitchen and heats frozen or prepared foods rather than cooks from scratch. Still other families may bring substitutions because they feel that it is important for their child to have these items instead of the ones that you serve. Items in this category are things such as organic products and "farm milk." The only real difference is a mistake under these conditions will not result in an ill child.

Children Who Bring Their Own Lunches

If you are serving meals, your policies should determine whether children are allowed to bring their own lunches or not. If you do allow these, determine and let parents know how you will handle food service for children who bring their own lunches. Also, specify what you will allow to be brought into the center.

There are some problems which can arise from children bringing their own lunches. These include: eating junk foods; starting trends that other children follow; wanting to eat both the lunch from home and the centers lunch; as well as wanting to choose favorites from the centers lunch and then eat them with their own lunch. Many of these problems create more of an overall center concern than a problem for the one child.

Policies which do not allow junk foods, desserts, and candy as part of a packed lunch will help support the health and nutrition of all of the children. The other children will most often also prefer junk food and sweets to the healthy lunch that you are providing. In addition, if some children begin to do this, you will see the "copy cat" versions coming quickly. You will see more and more children bringing junk food and sweets for their lunches. Be sure to state your policy on fast food brought to the center by parents as well. If you allow parents to bring in a lunch from a fast food restaurant for their child right at lunch time then that is fine. If you do not want parents dropping in with fast food lunches then be sure to note that on your policies.

❖ Lesson From the Field: Fast Food Policy

I excluded fast food lunches simply out of courtesy to the other children. Almost all of the children would rather eat the unhealthy lunch from a local fast food restaurant than a healthy lunch prepared for them. It smells good to everyone as it comes in the door. It comes with a toy and a soda. It's a nice treat on occasion; however, when planning for the health and feelings of the entire group of children it didn't seem appropriate to me. This was clearly stated in policies and rarely an issue.

Your policies must also address those extreme food allergies that some children can't come into contact with. An example is the peanut butter sandwich packed by one parent that comes into contact with a child who has a severe peanut allergy. Create policies and monitor the food brought into the center so that it isn't hazardous to other children.

One more area of policies and concern is food safety and reheating. Create policies that are feasible for your center and staff. Determine how you will store the lunches brought from home. Do you have room in your refrigerator? Will they need to pack the lunch box with ice packs? Will they bring the lunches already warm and then let it sit out for several hours. Obviously the safest method is to store it in your refrigerator at the appropriate temperature. If you have the ability to reheat food and choose to do so, that can be good for the children; however, be aware that this is very time consuming and will increase the time it takes to prepare lunches. Your staff members in the kitchen have to prepare the menu lunch plus go and heat up lunches for all of the children who brought lunches from home. If this is not feasible, make your policies clear that parents must send "ready to eat" lunches that do not require heating.

Parents may send lunches already warmed in a thermos. This can be a concern based on how long the food remains off temperature. Determine what is appropriate and safe. Make policies that work for you and protect the children. Then enforce those policies. Yes, some parents will complain when you enforce the policies. They don't understand the complexities of preparing and taking care of many small children at one time. Simply show the written policy or talk to them and let them know this is what you do. Your policies are written to produce the greatest benefits for all of your children.

❖ Lesson From the Field: Encouraging Healthy Food

I created and enforced healthy food policies. If children brought junk food in their lunches, then I had the employee preparing lunches leave it in the lunch box to go back home. Our policies also included putting the home prepared lunch on the same type of plate as the other children's lunches along with pouring the drink into the same type of cup. This eliminated the status of all the cute lunch boxes and didn't encourage more outside lunches. If your staff already prepares full lunches at the center, it is actually harder and more time consuming to go and prepare the individual lunches brought from home. Even though this is the case, some parents will ask for discounts because they bring their own food. I would never provide a discount, they were purchasing a packaged program and everything was included. It's not different from missing a day of class. We purchased and prepared enough food for all of the children and it was the parent's option if they chose to bring something else.

Be careful of trend setting, at one time yogurt became very popular. One child brought yogurt to go with his lunch. After that a few more children brought yogurt, and so on. We were opening many yogurt containers to supplement the lunches. This same type of issue arose when children actually brought lunches because it was fun to do even though they actually wanted the foods we were serving. This created a concept of inequity because we were letting them have all of their lunch and parts of the lunch we were serving as well. Then it wasn't fair for those who only had the center's lunch. Serving became quite cumbersome as teachers tried to pass out all of the regular foods; open all of the individual containers in those lunch boxes; refill cups with milk; refill cups with lactose free milk; and refill cups from multiple juice boxes from the lunch containers parents had sent.

At this point, I made a new policy and sent it home with all of the children. The children that brought their lunches would be served their lunches from home and the children who did not would be served the lunch from the menu. It streamlined the process and made it much more feasible. It also eliminated a large number of lunches brought from home. We went back to the real purpose of allowing lunches from home which was to allow an alternate lunch for children who didn't like the food on the menu.

Centers Which Do Not Provide Lunches

For centers which do not provide lunches, pay careful attention to the details discussed for children who bring their own lunches. Many of the concerns are still the same. You still have to be concerned with the quality of lunches, the copy cat effect, and severe food allergies. In addition, the concerns on food storage, safety, correct temperatures, and reheating foods are all relevant when it comes to lunch time for centers that do not have commercial kitchens.

"No Outside Food" Policies

Due to so many complications with food services and substitutions, some centers utilize a policy of "no outside food." This eliminates a number of concerns that were addressed regarding outside food. The center will still need policies to determine how they will deal with food allergies, religious restrictions on specified foods, and children who won't eat what is on the menu. These policies have to be clear to parents as they enroll children, so they can determine if these policies will work for them.

Purchasing Food

If you choose to have food service in your center, then you will also have the option of going and shopping for the food or having it delivered to your center. Factors used to determine which method is right for your center include: the cost of having the delivery made to you; food storage capacity; and the number of children that are enrolled in your program. Consider the cost and time associated with each option and determine which works best for your center.

An effective way to manage kitchen paper goods as well as all of the other basic consumables used at the center is getting a membership to a warehouse store. The savings can add up very quickly when you buy in bulk. This is very effective for reducing costs on items which can be kept for long periods of time and are used in great volume such as toilet paper, paper towels, disposable cups and plates, plastic eating utensils, hand soap, dish soap, and cleaning supplies. It is also effective for purchasing large cans of vegetables, boxes of cereal, and other food items which you will use in large volumes.

For routine grocery shopping, the least expensive method is usually to shop at a local discount store. You can pick up the groceries yourself or have an employee do this job for you. When you use this method you are able to comparison shop, choose store brands, and even use seasonal produce when it is on sale. The downside of this method is that it is time consuming. There is a cost to calculate based on the time it takes to go shopping and bring all of the groceries back to the center. In addition, you either have to do this part yourself or have an employee that you trust with a credit card or other means of payment.

Doing your own grocery shopping can be beneficial if you have limited storage space. This can be true of pantry space and especially true with respect to refrigerator and freezer space. Some centers may choose to purchase very large refrigerators and freezers. For smaller centers, it may be more cost and space efficient to have typical home sized appliances and shop more often.

In a large childcare center, the size of the center and the volume of shopping needed may justify the additional cost of having the groceries delivered. Many grocery delivery companies only provide name brand foods. This can be a consideration because, when this is the case, the option, of purchasing store brands or generic products, is not available. This will increase the food costs in addition to the increased cost of having the foods delivered. Depending on the frequency of the deliveries, additional storage space may be needed including large pantries along with commercial size refrigerators and freezers. In addition, pay close attention to the scheduling of perishable items such as fresh fruits, vegetables, and milk.

Take the time to evaluate the costs and the time associated with each method before choosing the one that is right. Also, go back and re-evaluate those costs from time to time. If your center enrollment grows over the years, the grocery delivery may be cost effective later when it wasn't in the early years. Don't forget to reevaluate your methods and change as your center changes.

Serving Food

How and where you will serve the food will be a relevant decision. Do you have a specified dining room or will you serve meals inside the classrooms? If you have a dining room, will you serve everyone in the same dining room? Will all of the children fit in the dining room at one time or will you need to have different lunch times? Just as when you are determining the best means for purchasing food, this decision will be largely based on how many children are enrolled along with the room layout of your center. As your enrollment grows over time, it may be necessary to adjust how and where lunches are served.

Lunch time can be one of the busiest and nosiest times of the day. This is particularly true with serving methods that utilize refilling food for children. Many children are talking. Other children need something at the same time. Children are requesting different things. The teachers have difficulty hearing and some children may be getting up to get their needs met. Creating an appropriate system for lunch time will change this atmosphere to a very good experience. There are numerous ways this can be accomplished; one of the best ways is to have children talk quietly. Let them know when they are too loud and have them get quiet again.

There are several ways that lunches can be served. You can serve a full plate of food with correct full portions based on the child's age and nutritional needs to each child (such as what is typically done in a school cafeteria). This method doesn't allow for refills. Another method is to serve a small serving of each item on the menu and then refill plates as children eat. A third method which has great popularity in theory is serving family style. Children have large serving dishes of food on the table. They serve themselves and then pass it to others as in a traditional family dinner setting.

❖ Lesson From the Field: Serving Lunches

I prefer the method of starting children with a small portion of each food on the menu. This inevitably ends up with less waste. Children who are going to throw away a particular food will throw away the small portion on their plate instead of the larger portion which would have been included in the first method. If they aren't going to eat it, it does little good to put more on the plate. Then the children who like that food will have even more in the form of refills.

It is very important to encourage children to try all of the different foods on their plate. This helps the children to try new healthy foods and learn to like new foods. It is also important to teach children not to say negative things about a particular food. This can lead to others "following" just because someone said it was "yucky" rather than eating a food. Children often follow and take cues from others both positive and negative. Help direct them in a positive way.

When refills are served, only serve one thing at a time. If they want more of the item that is being served, then they need to raise their hand. Everything will be refilled, but the children can wait for the item they want. It helps to eliminate the gulping down of food that some children will do to get more refills faster. Taking turns refilling only one item at a time gives children the time to slow down; try the other items on their plate while they wait for their favorite to be refilled; and it eliminates the need to yell out what they want.

Teachers serving children must be carefully trained in the areas of sanitation and food safety. These things don't always come automatically. Teachers must wash their hands before handling food. They must also wash their hands again if they do anything that could potentially spread germs while they are working in the kitchen. Examples of this include, touching their own face or hair, cleaning something off the floor, and wiping a child's nose or face.

Food must be served at a correct temperature for children. It must be brought up to the appropriate temperature for food safety; however, it's not a restaurant. Food must be allowed to cool down to a safe temperature for a small child before it is put in front of the child. Throughout the research, there are occasional citations for burns based on food being served at a temperature that was too hot for children. These are usually determined by a state investigation based on a parent who was upset because her child was burned by food that was too hot.

It is important that teachers have a full understanding of the issues of cross contamination when they are refilling children's plates. If the details aren't carefully explained, many teachers will refill plates incorrectly. While serving another helping, they will touch a child's plate with the serving utensil. This allows for cross contamination. The serving utensils must never touch a child's plate that has been eaten from. This creates issues of spreading germs from that child's plate back into the serving dish and onto the plates of other children.

Family style eating is wonderful in theory. It allows children to have a lunch just as they would at home with their family. Passing serving dishes around and using the serving spoon is a wonderful means for developing fine motor skills and learning to do things for themselves. However, this method of food service should be carefully evaluated prior to making it your method of meal service. Family style meals in a childcare center with many small children, unless very carefully monitored and assisted, are likely to provide extensive opportunities for cross contamination of the food. As small children do what small children do … wipe their noses, put their fingers in their mouths, sneeze, and cough; they present numerous opportunities to share their germs. Cross contamination happens easily as children pass the food; share the serving spoon; and let the serving spoon touch the food on their plate before putting it back into the serving bowls.

Always plan for more food than you must have. There are many things that happen in only a moment with small children. It is very common for children to drop an entire plate of food on the floor; have a friend reach over and eat off of their plate or drink from their cup; or spill their drink onto someone else's plate. Thankfully it's not often, but yes, children will even vomit onto a table where others are eating or all over the kitchen floor. Be ready to do whatever is necessary including tossing out food, sanitizing an entire area, and giving a new plate of food to all of the children impacted.

11

Staffing: Hiring, Releasing, and Retaining

In this chapter, you will explore the various components of effective staffing procedures including:

- Staffing Overview
- Creating a Hiring System that Works
- Experience vs. Inexperience
- Providing an Improvement Plan
- Immediate Firing
- Helping Employees Decide to Leave
- Employees Who's Performance Deteriorates Over Time
- Retaining Good Staff Members
- Risks Associated with Employees Leaving
- Parents Who Want to Work at the Center
- Physical Fitness as a Job Qualification
- Staff Turnover
- Other Staffing Realities

Staffing Overview

Hiring the right staff is a vitally important part of a successful center. The caregivers are your front lines. These are the people that greet the parents at the door; care for the children; and carry out your day to day operations. The more successful your center becomes the less ability you have to be everywhere. You depend on your staff to carry out the vision and quality of your center. A quality staff that carries out your wishes by providing a wonderful atmosphere, a safe environment, excellent childcare, and parental support is a true asset to your business. Just the opposite is true if the quality of staff is poor.

As in all areas of the childcare business, make a point to understand the applicable laws in this area. Know the applicable national and state laws and carefully comply with all employment laws. In addition, make sure that all of your personnel policies and procedures meet the regulations for childcare in your state including age and education requirements.

Creating a Hiring System that Works

In the summer of 2007, I filled the same position four times. Hiring and keeping good staff is one of the most difficult challenges of managing a childcare center. At that point, I knew that my process had to change and include insight into more elements.

A good hiring process for childcare should contain multiple steps, including such things as the application, phone screening, interview, and an on-site evaluation. Having a multiple step process will allow you to see the prospective employee several times and assess her accordingly. The simple ability for a person to show up, dressed presentable, and on time is in itself a test. It can be amazing, how many applicants will simply not show up to a second interview or on site evaluation. This is the same person who wouldn't have shown up to work on the first or second day.

The first step is to actively seek out good candidates. This can include print advertising; posting a sign on your property or door; word of mouth through both parents and staff members; and other methods. Collect as many applications and resumes as possible. Having a larger applicant pool can provide access to more qualified candidates. There are things beyond your control and at times, you may receive a great number of applicants for a position while at other times you may continue to seek out candidates for some time with fewer applicants. Once you have chosen some applicants that look good on paper, it's time for the next step.

The next step is a telephone screening. Call the applicants who appear promising and ask them some simple open ended questions. It is amazing the information you can obtain from a simple telephone screening. At this point you are able to determine if this is someone that you want to call in for an interview or if it is someone who would not be a good fit in your organization. Don't hire from a telephone call ... it is a screening. It simply eliminates those who you are certain will not make a good fit for your organization and position. Doing it this way saves a great deal of time for you and the applicant (who ultimately wouldn't get the job anyway).

I had one phone screening in which I was asked: "Those three year olds are potty trained and don't wear diapers, right?" My conclusion was that she wasn't willing to change diapers. She wasn't someone I needed to interview. I wouldn't hire anyone who wouldn't change a diaper. Even if working with preschool age children was her regular position, it didn't guarantee that she wouldn't be placed in a toddler room if I needed her there on a particular day. In addition, the more obvious fact is that many children all the way into school-age continue to have occasional accidents. Newsflash: These are children! Keeping them clean and assisting them by whatever means is necessary is part of the job. Phone screenings can be very revealing. It's amazing what people will share with you!

Staffing: Hiring, Releasing, and Retaining

❖ Lesson From the Field: Sharing Too Much

> *One applicant over the phone elaborated when asked whether she had any criminal convictions. She said yes, it was 20 years ago and she was young and had a controlled substance in her car. She went on with more details such as "I am clean; I haven't drank in 2 years." Anyone who continues and talks like this would be talking like that to all of the parents as well and certainly didn't have the personality requirements I needed. In addition, she moved an issue from 20 years ago into something within the last 2 years.*

Watch out for Red Flags: Proceed with caution when your phone screenings of a candidate include sharing information such as:

- ✓ Issues with her own child at the center where she used to work
- ✓ Issues with management, other staff members, or parents from the center where she used to work
- ✓ Issues with personal injuries occurring at a center where she used to work
- ✓ Sharing negative information about the center where she used to work

From the phone conversation, you can get a very clear picture of whether or not this is someone you are interested in learning more about. Keep in mind that if she has negative things to say about her former childcare employer that she will likely have the same issues with you if hired. Although some issues really are relevant to a particular employer, many issues are grounded in the individual's way of seeing things and are likely to be repeated. Also, the willingness to openly talk negatively about an employer should be a concern for you as a potential employer. You need dedicated employees who are able to retain confidential information both in regards to the children and to your center as a whole.

Use whatever questions would help you decide if you want to ask this person to come in and interview. (Prepare questions after making sure you understand what you are legally allowed to ask and what questions are not permitted based on labor laws.) Even more than the specific questions, it is simply the ability to have the candidate talk to you. Ask open ended questions and listen. You will get a good feel for the person and if she might make a good employee.

If the person sounds like a good candidate, you can then ask her to come in for an interview. If not, then let her know that you are talking to other people. Tell her you will get back in touch with her and politely end the conversation. (You will then get back with her when you send out all of your letters saying that you hired someone who is a better match for the position.)

Interviews are the next step. As she arrives for an interview, evaluate the following:

- ✓ Does she arrive on time?
- ✓ How does she present herself as she enters?
- ✓ How does she speak to your current staff?
- ✓ Are her clothing and appearance appropriate for your center?
- ✓ Does she exude obvious odors (such as body odors or a heavy smoke smell)?
- ✓ Does she have body piercings or tattoos that are displayed openly?

Remember, you are choosing someone to work with your children and present the image of your center. You determine what is acceptable. Whatever your criteria is, fully assess how this person measures up to that criteria.

There are many sources for interview questions. (Remember to make sure that your questions are legal, based on employment laws.) Choose those that are most likely represent what you will need for your particular center and the age group that you are hiring a teacher for. Over time you will create your own set which correlates really well to what you need for a good employee. I recommend your questions go much further than the typical interview questions. After you have completed those questions consider some of mine.

The following are some of the questions that I always included in interviews:

- ✓ Are you willing to clean up diarrhea?
- ✓ Are you willing to clean up children who have potty accidents? (This can be much messier than simply changing diapers.)
- ✓ Are you willing to clean up vomit off the floor?
- ✓ Are you willing to clean toilets?
- ✓ Are you willing to mop floors?
- ✓ Are you willing to wash dishes and clean the kitchen?

Clearly this isn't what they were thinking when they applied to work in a childcare center; however, this is the real world of childcare. It is filled with realities far beyond working with adorable children coloring pictures and playing. Candidates don't think about some of these things that are guaranteed to be a part of working with small children

Make sure that potential employees will do the required work because these are realities. When they are hesitant at the thought of the unpleasant questions, it is an opportunity to understand that these individuals will probably not work out well. Interviews can be very revealing.

I experienced many odd situations while interviewing including:

- ✓ A woman who brought her boyfriend to the interview for support
- ✓ Candidates who brought their children with them and then couldn't control them during the interview
- ✓ Numerous candidates who smelled heavily of cigarette smoke odor and the odor stayed much longer than the candidates
- ✓ Inappropriate dress, tattoos, and body piercings

I would advise adding one more step to your process. This step is an observational interview. I added it to our process in later years and found it to be very beneficial in making the decision to hire someone. The observational interview included having the candidate show up in work appropriate dress and work with a lead teacher in the classroom where you would be expecting her to work if hired.

The observational interview allows you to evaluate some simple concepts as well as how she might work in the classroom. This step allows you to observe one more time whether this person would show up and be on time. You may be surprised at how many fail on this end. Before implementing this step, I had a number of new hires who just never showed up on their first scheduled day of work. Not that I can guarantee it will work every time, but all of my teachers who completed this step did actually show up to work on the first day.

I devised a scoring sheet where the lead teacher would rate the job candidate on a number of relevant details that she was able to observe. This allowed experienced teachers input into the process. They were provided a say in who would be working with them. The director will always have the final say but having others provide input is valuable. It gives insight into whether the candidate would be able to work well with your existing staff. When you are certain that you have someone you want to extend an offer to, determine what you can pay her; her work schedule; and prepare to make an offer.

The offer phone call should confer the following information:

- ✓ The Position
- ✓ Job Description
- ✓ Start Date
- ✓ Work Schedule
- ✓ Pay Rate
- ✓ Date to Complete Required Personnel Paperwork
- ✓ Contingency Statement

Make sure that you state the job offer is contingent on meeting all of the requirements for hiring. Depending on your state regulations, this can include passing background checks and fingerprinting, along with providing appropriate documentation such as: identification; social security or work permits; certification for CPR and first aid; and completing all hiring paperwork.

The person may accept on the spot or may need to think about it. In the second scenario, set a deadline for her to call you back and let you know. Be very up front and let the candidate know that if you do not hear from her by a specific date and time, you will assume she has chosen not to accept the position and you will hire someone else. This is important because you can't hold up your process for someone indefinitely no matter how good you think she might be.

❖ Lesson From the Field: Don't Wait on a Candidate

I had one particular candidate that I was absolutely convinced would make a valued employee. She was mature, had a professional appearance and seemed extremely dedicated to her work at another childcare center. In fact she was so dedicated that I waited a few weeks to even get her in for an interview. She could never get off work. After she finally passed the interview stage, I waited until she could give her employer lots of time to find a replacement. Then I waited for her to take care of some personal matters. Finally she started work ... that was also her last day of work. She had even more concerns that took precedence at that point and she wasn't able to come back to work.

After that, the lesson was learned: Never wait on someone. If you hire a new employee, do allow her the ability to provide an appropriate notice to her current employer. However, don't wait if she can't make it into an interview in a timely manner; can't start work within a reasonable time frame; or makes other excuses for delays.

If the candidate accepts the job then the next step is to schedule a time for the candidate to come in and complete the paperwork. The paperwork should include permission to run background checks plus scheduling fingerprinting if required. Complete all of the required paperwork and schedule background checks at this time. Also be sure to provide the employee with a written job description and beginning pay rate and have her sign it.

Hire carefully, there are only two options for hiring someone who is not good for your center. You have to either fire her or live with her until she chooses to leave. Neither of these is a good option. Take your time and be sure. Yes, that means that at times you will work longer hours and you will have your current staff members working long hours. This is a better option than hiring someone who is not good for your children and your business. Careful hiring reduces turnover in an industry known for high turnover, low wages, huge responsibilities, and high stress for workers. The time needed for a complete hiring process is a very good investment that will pay off over time with better employees and less turnover.

It often took me six weeks to hire a good candidate. Over time, I learned to take my time and use the process. It usually paid off with good employees but it was often challenging as we worked with a smaller staff than desired for a period of time. Even when the employee who was leaving provided a two week notice, this still left us short for weeks. It was better to work with a really good staff and reward them accordingly than to hire quickly and have less than desirable employees. There were even times when I couldn't fill a position with someone I wanted, so I increased overtime and hours of good employees and chose not to hire for awhile.

After you have completed the hiring process, it is a good policy to send a letter out to all of the applicants who were not hired. Create a professional letter, which simply states that you hired someone who better met the qualifications of the position and that you wish them the best in their employment search. It's simple, to the point, and it provides the common courtesy of letting each applicant know that she is no longer under consideration. There are a number of books of letters as well as internet examples which can come in handy when you are looking for standardized letters to meet such needs and do not want to compose your own.

Consider the possibility of hiring part-time rather than full-time. Many people require a full-time position, making it necessary to provide those hours in order to hire the right person. However, hiring two part-time employees instead of one full-time can provide great benefits. Often part-time positions become full-time positions over time. Almost always, when I hired two people, one would not work out in the long term. Usually someone would leave. Often finding out that this work was much more difficult than she would ever have thought. Hiring two part-time employees allows for the most successful employee to work into full time. It also means it is easier to adjust employee schedules if one doesn't work out. It's much easier to cover a part-time position that doesn't work than a full-time one.

Experience vs. Inexperience

Hiring experienced staff members means you hired employees that "know what they are getting into." They know the difficulty of the job and that they enjoy working with children ... even with the ups and downs. However, they often have preconceived ideas of how things should be done and will not always buy into your way of doing things.

Hiring staff without experience is different. Often these employees do not understand the level of demands associated with a job in childcare. Many will find that it is not for them. When you hire employees who are new to the field and they love the work, it can be a wonderful match. The benefits of hiring these new employees is that they are generally open to all of your ideas and training without preconceived notions.

❖ Lesson From the Field: Hiring Experience Isn't Always Better

I interviewed a candidate who worked at All Day Childcare, a center that was open from early morning until well past midnight on a regular basis. I asked questions regarding Texas minimum standards and she wasn't familiar with the regulations. She explained that she kept six infants alone (Texas standards allowed four). She worked alone, late at night. She put the children to sleep and then cleaned up dinner leaving them alone in the room. She never saw the director or even knew who she was. She had paid $40.00 for her background check but her fingerprints were never completed. In this case, experience wasn't a plus.

You went through all the steps; did everything according to your plans; hired the person and then he isn't working out. This should be rare, but it does happen. The multi-step process helps you know the person better than just using an interview; however, the hiring process is still not perfect. You don't fully know a person and how he will perform on the job, until he is there with you. It can take a few weeks before he becomes comfortable and you are really able to see how well he fits (or doesn't fit) into your center.

Providing an Improvement Plan

Once you have determined that an employee is not a good fit for your childcare center, you have to determine if you will release her or allow her to stay on. Let the person know what she is not doing correctly. Create a plan for improvement and attempt to help her with her performance. Get it all in writing and have the employee sign the document each time. If the employee refuses to sign, make a note at the bottom of the document that she refuses to sign it. Provide deadlines for improvement and allow the person to correct her performance short falls. If these aren't corrected, then you can release her from duty. (As in all major decisions, know the laws associated with such actions.)

Immediate Firing

Very seldom is it necessary to fire someone on the spot; however, at times you may deem this necessary. This can be the case when someone is completely out of line in their behaviors and are absolutely not suitable to be on site at your center. The safety and environment for the children is absolutely paramount. When a staff member violates these areas, immediate release may be warranted. Just be prepared that this is not a good situation; it will likely have some ongoing consequences. Take the time to correctly document the circumstances of the firing. The documentation should include the date, time, and provide a factual recount of all relevant details that led to the firing. (Know your state laws regarding the release of employees.) Be prepared as this may lead to an unemployment claim that you will need to defend later. If the situation involved other employees or parents, it is a good idea to take down their statements as well. Have all of this ready if you are contacted regarding the release of the employee.

Helping Employees Decide to Leave

One of the most valuable tools to use is that of counseling and talking to an employee who is not working out. This usually occurs in newer hires that for various reasons are just not showing good performance. Often it is evident to the individual as well. She may not be happy with the work. Many new employees come to this point of reality when the real world of childcare doesn't meet their expectations of a fun filled happy world.

In such situations, it is good to sit down with the employee. You should discuss the particular behaviors and performance issues which are not meeting your expectations. Then take time to listen. Let her tell you why those things are happening. As with all staffing concerns, be open to providing assistance and an improvement plan if she wants to continue. Also listen for indications that she is frustrated and it isn't working for her either. If those types of conversations are surfacing, then you can bring up concepts that help her know that it is okay to decide this is not the right place for her.

❖ Lesson From the Field: Helping Someone Decide to Quit

After making good impressions during the hiring process, my new teacher had come to work looking very bad. She said she was sick and so I let her go home and told her to return for her very important CPR training that evening. She didn't return and couldn't be contacted. She had slept through the CPR training. Following this, she fell asleep while she was supposed to be supervising the nap room; overslept twice when she was supposed to be there at 6:30 AM; wore inappropriate clothing; answering her personal cell phone while in the classroom; and was caught talking on her cell phone while watching children on the playground. She then texted me one evening to say she wanted to discuss personnel issues at our upcoming staff meeting. It was clear that she hadn't been here long enough to have issues and she wasn't a model preschool teacher. I simply replied "see me." She had only worked at the center for two weeks and had a large list of documented problems.

The next morning she was upset and needed to talk. She didn't feel she was treated fairly by other employees. She wasn't sure this is where she needed to be. I took the opportunity to say she could resign now and it would be fine. I made her feel better about leaving. It was clearly best for both of us and quite frankly my opportunity to "help her leave" so that it wasn't necessary to fire her.

Part with employees amicably if at all possible. If it's not working, the employee will usually feel it as well and likely be frustrated and unhappy. Help her by taking away the guilt, let her know its ok, and try to leave it all on good terms. If possible, because at this point it is her choice, ask her to write a brief resignation letter for your documentation that she is choosing to leave.

In the years of operating my center, I actually fired very few individuals. It wasn't necessary as most of the time when I took time to listen. The reason that the job performance wasn't up to my expectations was due to the fact that the employee wasn't happy. Most often employees were relieved to understand that I wasn't angry and they had my well wishes if they wanted to move on. Sometimes this would result in an immediate resignation, other times this would mean the individual would be there a little longer as she looked for another job that better suited her.

Employees Who's Performance Deteriorates Over Time

The most difficult performance problems and choices often center on employees who were really good performers at one time but have progressively gotten worse over a number of years. This doesn't happen often but it does happen. There are a number of things that can contribute to this including burn out, and employees who are ready to move on but haven't been able to find other employment. These are the hardest to manage, because they are no longer happy to be at work and yet they haven't been able to find something else they want.

Indications that a Staff Member is "Heading Downhill" include:

- ✓ Lack of enthusiasm
- ✓ Negative attitude
- ✓ Consistent issues with the work, team members, management
- ✓ Dress code violations
- ✓ Increased or excessive absences

Most of the time, these employees need support and understanding. They will eventually find what they need to move on; however, employees who are no longer happy in their work can create morale problems as well as work issues. In each case, you must decide if you will wait it out or if the situation has deteriorated enough that you need to release her from duty. If you choose to allow her to stay, then just as with new employees, she should be put on a performance improvement plan and provided assistance in how she can improve her job performance.

Many employees do have issues from time to time with everything from schedules, co-workers, their own children at your center, and other such things. Working with employees through listening to concerns or making a minor adjustment from time to time may be appropriate and beneficial. Be aware of those employees who constantly have issues. Fixing issues repeatedly becomes a problem. Such staff members are unhappy and are looking for and creating problems. Continuing to fix problems just enables them and creates a situation which drains your time and energy. The staff member needs to deal with her current work environment or choose to find another one. As the manager, on occasions, you may find it necessary to point this out to an employee and choose not to fix issues for her.

The best situations with respect to employees who are ready to move on include those staff members who recognize that fact and then provide appropriate notice. They leave on good terms and with good feelings toward their experience. It is even common for some of these employees to return to work at the center one day. Staff members who did a good job, left appropriately, and on good terms can make great future employees. They walk back in and know exactly what to do without all the training required for most new hires. These same employees who left with a positive attitude continue to provide good "word of mouth" for your business. They talk to others about the center and how good it is even after they no longer work there.

It isn't beneficial to keep staff members after they are tired of working in childcare. It is a demanding and stressful job. When a teacher is ready to leave the field of early childhood, it is best to wish her well in her new choice.

❖ Lesson From the Field: Letting Employees Go

I watched it happen repeatedly as staff members who were good at one time became tired and less valuable. They were ready to move on to something different. My motto that I often repeated was that I was happy to have them as long as they really wanted to be there and were doing good things for the children. At the point where they no longer wanted to be in childcare, my job was to wish them well in their future work. This time comes for many workers in this business. I wasn't happy to see good staff members leave, but they had their own lives and time frames. It was important for them to be able to move on with good wishes from me.

As a final step in the exiting process of an employee, be sure to complete and retain documentation. If you fired someone for cause, document the situation. If the employee was on an improvement plan, be sure to keep all the records along with the meetings of what was discussed and what was not corrected. If the employee chose to leave, have her write a simple letter of resignation which states her last day and that she is resigning. This statement documents that the choice was made by the employee. File those records and retain them in case they are needed at a later date.

Don't be surprised after releasing someone if you get a call from your state unemployment office because the former employee has filed an unemployment claim against you. This is where the documentation comes in. You need to be able to prove that you took appropriate steps to allow the person to improve their performance. Even in "employment-at-will" states, such as Texas, the documentation is important because former employees can still file unemployment claims. These funds, depending on circumstances and laws, can be "charged back" to you and essentially raise your unemployment taxes.

❖ Lesson From the Field: Unemployment Claims

Over the entire span of owning a childcare center, I never had an unemployment claim approved based on the release of an employee. I did have a few former employees file for unemployment. These included an employee who had quit because she was going to another town to take care of an ailing parent. It even included an employee who was fired on the spot for screaming and using inappropriate language towards another employee while in a classroom with children. I had to answer the questions and provide appropriate documentation related to each case. Each time, I won the case as the claims representative sided with me and denied the unemployment claim based on the documentation provided.

Retaining Good Staff Members

Retaining good staff members is as important as hiring them. As discussed, good staff members are the foundation of your ongoing success. Keeping staff members with good performance and experience in your center is a vital part of ongoing operation success. There are a number of strategies to utilize in keeping good staff members.

Knowing that typically childcare is an industry with low wages, make sure that your wages for your good employees are competitive. Also include regular performance evaluations and raises as a part of your long term strategy. Create your own evaluation and long term performance practices which provide support, ongoing training, and pay increases. Also include opportunities to sit down with your staff members to let them know that they are doing a great job and give them an opportunity to let you know what they need to continue to be motivated and progress professionally in their work.

Public recognition can be a great motivator. Be sure to not only let the staff member who is doing a great job know this, but make it public information. Simple rewards such as a t-shirt, candy, gift certificates, or special materials for their classroom can let that person's accomplishments be recognized by others as well. It is the "thank you" that is important. Do something that says "I appreciate all you do for the center." This can also create an environment where others want to accomplish more and receive that same recognition. Employees who work hard deserve to be given praise and recognition. It also creates a positive work environment. (As a side note, it is always a good idea to check with your CPA regarding any tax implications of rewards you provide to employees.)

Creating a positive work environment is an important way to retain good employees. A positive atmosphere; support for the employees needs; along with a director who listens to concerns and acts when appropriate are all ways to increase work satisfaction and keep good employees. The sad part is that you will not want everyone to stay. Make sure that your recognition and compensation strategies support the needs of your business. All policies should be fair and implemented consistently for all, but do not reward behaviors and personnel who have not earned the rewards. Provide the raises and rewards to those who have earned them.

While you are working on your retaining strategies, make sure that you are also putting long term planning to work. Consider who your most valuable staff members are and create plans for how you will make adjustments if they leave. It is inevitable that some of your best employees will leave at some point. Create opportunities for training and increasing skills for your staff. Know who you would move into a position if someone left. Create long term plans and alternative strategies for staffing situations. Don't be caught off guard and find yourself struggling to cope when you lose a valuable employee.

It is best, if at all possible, for your employees to move up within your own organization. Use the preparation discussed to have someone ready for movement. Hiring outside for higher level positions is risky in a number of ways. No matter how well fit a new employee appears to be, without a history of working for you, it is difficult to be sure that she will be good in a position which requires a great deal of responsibility. In addition, hiring from outside for your higher level positions, is an inherent sign to current employees that they will not be chosen for such positions. It can be a morale and retention issue for those already in your employment.

Risks Associated with Employees Leaving

A part of all initial paperwork should be a non-compete agreement. It should also include information that the curriculum and policies may not be shared with others outside of the organization. A real concern would be when good employees leave and take your information with them to someone else in the local area. Get this non-compete agreement in writing. I've seen times when an employee of a particular center would use his own name and reputation to start a new center in the same area. This change can then lead to pulling children and families from the established center into his new center. Such situations have the potential to have great consequences on the center which used to employ the teacher. A non-compete agreement should prevent such occurrences. This agreement should be signed by all employees when they are hired and it should specify exact terms, such as within how broad of an area and for what time period the individual is not to open a childcare center. The same is true if you are using a custom curriculum. This is intellectual property of the organization and is not to be taken or used outside of the center. This obviously doesn't apply to "off the shelf" curriculum that anyone can purchase.

It is more likely that employees will go to work for someone else in the local area than start their own business nearby. The concerns here center on the sharing of critical information about your center, your curriculum, and how you operate with another center. This is particularly true if you are a leader in your area and others attempt to duplicate your methods. This situation is harder to manage, but having employees sign a paper that states your curriculum, policies, and procedures are not to be shared is valuable. As employees are leaving, remind them of the agreements they signed, such as non-complete and confidentiality agreements.

Parents Who Want to Work at the Center

It is relatively common to have a parent of an enrolled child who wants to work at your center. Sometimes it can be a good thing and sometimes not. As a parent, of a center that carefully takes care of children and families, she may not always understand the realities of what it takes to get all of this done and done well. It looks easy but clearly it is very hard work.

❖ Lesson From the Field: When It's Not a Good Match

One parent wanted to "rock babies" when she found out I was putting in an infant room. Working in a licensed infant room was much more complicated than her vision of the work. In addition, she was a parent who was very particular and on more than one occasion had issues with us. Clearly it was not a good match.

❖ Lesson From the Field: Great Parents Can Make Great Teachers

I did hire a number of parents over the years. Many did a phenomenal job! They were parents of enrolled children first, so they "bought into" our way of doing things. Many had looked at other places and wouldn't even consider them for their child. These parents clearly brought a level of expertise and benefit to our center.

It's something to be analyzed considerably and cautiously. When it is right it can be an absolutely wonderful situation. When it's not right, you will likely have many problems brought into your center or lose the child enrolled as well as an employee. There is a detailed discussion of teachers and their own children together at the center in Chapter 15: Teachers and Their Own Children.

Physical Fitness as a Job Qualification

Make no mistake. This is a physical job! The physical requirements of the job are significant but may not be obvious at first to someone applying for the job. A common misconception is that working with small children means coming in, plopping down into a chair, and watching them play. Working with very young children in a quality licensed environment requires physical stamina.

The job requires a great deal of physical stamina including:

- ✓ Picking up children (many are not light)
- ✓ Getting up and down frequently
- ✓ Sitting on the floor with children
- ✓ Doing activities
- ✓ Actively working with children
- ✓ Running to stop a biting incident, prevent an accident, or handle an emergency
- ✓ Extensive cleaning activities

❖ Lesson From the Field: Physical Fitness Requirements

I distinctly remember a number of candidates who for various reasons had great difficulty walking to my office on the second floor. One candidate even told me that she was applying because she wanted to "slow down." It was very obvious that she would not be able to do the job based on the physical requirements of the work.

Be careful and adhere to all laws regarding job applicants, but the person must be able to physically do the job. What is even worse is hiring someone who can't physically do the work ... then what? Hiring someone who is not physically able to do the work can place children at risk. Your options are really bad at that point.

Staff Turnover

In my experience everything would be smooth for some time. I would have a full staff that had gained the necessary experience and was able to manage their classrooms, follow regulations, and were wonderful with children. Then there were other times when it seemed that multiple staff members wanted to leave at the same time. The rest of the staff would work very long hours as I spent a great deal of effort seeking out new employees to start the training process over again. This seemed even more dramatic many years as summer got closer. It's as if the staff got "spring fever" too and many were ready to make a change.

Things that can't be changed should be used as opportunities. It's an opportunity to move deserving staff into higher positions with pay increases. It also provides an opportunity to find new people who are enthusiastic about joining the team. I always tried to start new teachers out at a lower pay rate with part-time hours in order to allow them to prove themselves. If the pay is lower and not increased, they are likely to leave and sometimes you want that. Some turnover is positive. It allows you to increase hours and pay for your high performers while allowing low performers to "choose" to move on. These policies create a higher performing staff overall.

On a couple of occasions I hired absolutely wonderful people and it still didn't work. It can be a very disappointing event when you have staff members who are doing a wonderful job, want to work for you, but due to life circumstances beyond their control they leave with little or no warning.

❖ Lesson From the Field: It's a Great Match and it Still Doesn't Work

I definitely felt like I hired the right person. Ms. Smith was hired for a part-time afternoon position with the possibility of extending to full time hours if her performance proved worthy. She came in able to handle children well, very nice, trying really hard, and expressing how happy she was to be with us.

One day she just didn't show up to work. She came in the following day very upset that their living situation with a family member wasn't working and they had to move out. Her family was going to live with another relative but for only a short time. They weren't sure what

was in store after that since they had no money, no phone, and no vehicle. I got on my computer and printed out her paycheck for all of the hours she had worked so she would have some money. She said that she would call me on Friday (in two days) and let me know where things stood. She never called. She had stayed less than 2 months.

There are also times when teachers leave without any notice at lunch or simply don't show up to work again. Sometimes you know what happened to initiate the event and sometimes you really don't.

Some incidents I experienced included:

- ✓ A wonderful teacher provided notice of a death in the family. She requested two days off and never returned to work.
- ✓ A new teacher left at lunch after a disagreement with a lead teacher on how to administer a child's asthma medicine. She never returned.
- ✓ An established staff member didn't "feel like getting up and going to work." A few days later she inquired to another staff member to ask about her job to which I responded: "I don't believe she has a job here anymore."

Other Staffing Realities

Staffing realities can extend beyond the expected. Over time you will see your share of routinely occurring events along with some surprising things that you would have preferred to have been left out.

Some staffing realities include:

- ✓ Collection calls to the business looking for staff members
- ✓ Difficult events regarding their own children and families
- ✓ Arrests for minor offenses (such as unpaid traffic tickets)
- ✓ Investigations of various forms
- ✓ Concerns about vehicle repossessions occurring at the workplace

The collection calls are likely the most frequent thing that you will have to deal with. Once a collection agency has your number, you can expect volumes of phone calls, many just recordings as they try to track people down. These callers are looking to track down current employees, former employees, and even people you've never seen, much less employed. Don't let these disturb your employees focus; you don't need to provide any information. Tell them they need to locate a personal number that this is a business and you have work to do. It may be an issue but it isn't your issue and it doesn't belong in your business.

12

Staff Training

In this chapter, you will learn the important areas of focus for staff training including:

- Staff Training Overview
- Establishing Basic Rules
- Professionalism and Staff Dress Code
- Duties and Responsibilities
- Classroom Management
- Teaching Skills
- Liability Issues and Teachers
- Policy Meetings to Update and Remind

Staff Training Overview

Initial paperwork should have been completed as a part of the hiring process and background checks. This should all be done prior to bringing an employee into the organization. Have the employees complete and sign any remaining employment paperwork, such as job descriptions and non-compete agreements at the beginning of the training process.

The training program should include classroom study on policies, procedures, state regulations, and overall expectations. It should also include hands-on training with one of your best teachers or with multiple teachers. A comprehensive training program is essential to developing a valuable employee and to the safety and care of the children. Never give a new employee responsibility over a group of children without fully preparing her for the work.

Establishing Basic Rules

Set your rules for absenteeism and tardiness. How will you manage breaks and who covers classes while the teachers take breaks? Will you have a floater (someone who goes between classes to assist)? Establish policies for eating and drinking while on the job, restroom breaks, lunch breaks, and cell phone usage.

It is very important that these rules are carefully thought out. An often noted philosophy is to just fire someone who doesn't comply. I've heard this many times at management seminars and in managerial philosophies; however, I never had a line of well qualified people waiting to jump in when I fired someone.

This is often not the best choice. As with all policies, think it through. How are you going to respond when one of your absolute best teachers just can't ever seem to make it to work on time? Make sure you layout policies that you will be able to enforce and implement them consistently among all of your staff.

Professionalism and Staff Dress Code

The appearance of your staff makes an impression either positive or negative. It is important to establish and maintain appropriate appearances for your childcare business. Set your policies to demonstrate a professional atmosphere. This may very well be based on your center's concept, philosophy, and goals. Always err on the side of conservative when making such appearance policies.

Keep in mind that you expect a professional appearance and yet the staff will be working in many capacities that can be rough on clothing including markers, paint, cleaners, and even dirt from outside. It was predictable; every so often one of my staff members would ruin a shirt or pants by getting bleach on their clothing. Do expect employees to look professional; however, let them know that they shouldn't wear expensive clothing to work. They can look nice and still wear relatively inexpensive clothing.

Clothing considerations should include details such as:

- ✓ Will you use a standardized dress code?
- ✓ Will you provide school shirts for each employee?
- ✓ Are shorts allowed? If yes, what length is required?
- ✓ Are staff members allowed to wear open toed shoes or flip flops?
- ✓ Are staff members allowed to remove their shoes inside the classroom?
- ✓ How will you specify necklines for staff members? (Remember teachers are bending over picking up children not just sitting at a desk. This impacts the way clothes look and how much is revealed.)
- ✓ Are jeans allowed? If so are there any requirements regarding fading, holes, and torn fabric?

- ✓ How low can pants and jeans sit on the waist? What is appropriate for the bending and active movement of the job?
- ✓ Are tattoos allowed in sight or required to be covered?
- ✓ Are body piercings and body jewelry (other than earrings) allowed?

If your policies include providing shirts with your center's name on it, make sure to specify professionalism standards while wearing the shirt. Anytime they are seen in the shirt, staff members can be connected to the center. This means that while they are wearing the shirt they should have behavior appropriate to represent the center. Examples include prohibiting drinking and bad language while wearing the shirt.

Make your policies according to the atmosphere you are working to create, and then be ready to enforce those requirements. It can feel like you are the clothing police, but what is not corrected is understood as implied permission. If one person wears something that is not appropriate according to your dress code, address it. If it is significant send her home to change clothes. If you don't correct the dress code violation, expect others to follow with the excuse that "someone else does it." Does it sound juvenile? Yes, but it is a predictable circumstance.

Duties and Responsibilities

There are so many duties and responsibilities within the center. As noted in earlier chapters, these include more than working with children. Unless you hire someone specifically to clean all day, it is necessary to incorporate such duties into the schedule of your staff members.

Cleaning duties other than those necessary for picking up after the children are generally required to be done by a staff member who is "not included in the child to staff ratio" required by state standards. Make sure that you have included enough staff in your schedule to accommodate the necessary cleaning while continuing to maintain the required ratios.

Good times to implement these duties include outdoor playtime, naptime, and closing time where you can usually have an increased ratio (assuming you are maintaining a lower ratio during class time) and still have an appropriate state required level of supervision. At appropriate times such as these, have cleaning assignments for staff members and allow them time to do those outside of time they are responsible for the children.

The more specific the cleaning and duty assignments are, the better. At times it is necessary to create some rather detailed cleaning charts because it is amazing what doesn't get done if it isn't specifically spelled out as part of the assignment. Examples include: cleaning the kitchen but not cleaning the dishes; not including floors in the task of cleaning the room; missing the toilet when cleaning the bathroom; and other such things.

It seems obvious what should be included and when you have well trained, diligent and experienced staff it can be. When you are working with less experienced and less competent staff (such as times when your most experienced teachers are with the children or at lunch) and you leave the cleaning duties to your more novice employees, you will often find things are not done to your standards. Even after creating charts, working with staff, and ongoing supervision, you will find that some employees are simply not that capable or not interested in completing such tasks well.

Classroom Management

As I hired teachers who were new to the field of childcare, I did extensive training in classroom management and let them know that mastering classroom management is for most individuals the hardest part of the work. Include sufficient training in how to handle various situations appropriately. Make sure to allow new teachers time to work inside classrooms with experienced teachers who actively represent the classroom management skills that you want in your center. Make sure that your staff is fully trained in your appropriate and licensed approved methods for discipline. Also, this reiterates the need to be actively involved in staff supervision and ensure that your teachers are managing their classrooms as you have instructed.

Managing groups of children in a positive and helpful manner can be very challenging. Based on the type of childcare establishment, the methodology can vary from a loud play atmosphere all the way to a very quiet classroom and learning atmosphere. Choose the method that is right for your center's concept and train your new staff well. Explain the methodology during the study portion of the training then proceed to hands-on training. Most of the real understanding of how to manage the classroom will come from working with an experienced teacher.

Areas of classroom management to address include:

- ✓ How children are expected to behave
- ✓ How the expectations are relayed to the children
- ✓ How teachers are to reinforce rules to children when they are broken
- ✓ Schedules
- ✓ Changing activities to hold children's interest
- ✓ Transition activities

Good Classroom Management Techniques Include:

- ✓ Talking to the child
- ✓ Re-directing the child
- ✓ A brief period of time out
- ✓ Removal from the classroom (into an alternate supervised situation)
- ✓ Assistance from the director
- ✓ Parent note home
- ✓ Phone call to the parent

When these and other appropriate state approved disciplinary measures do not work, then it is time to involve the parents. In a worst case scenario where a child is truly beyond the control of the center, the parent should be called to come and take the child home. If this is a recurring problem, and you are not able to manage the child's behavior within these correct disciplinary measures, then the child should be dismissed from the program. Under no circumstances should you progress into other methods which are not appropriate even if provided permission by the parents. Yes, I've had parents tell me to just "take a belt to him." The answer is no! It not only violates my own belief in what is appropriate discipline it clearly doesn't hold up to appropriate regulatory criteria. You must always utilize appropriate discipline or have the child removed from your center either for the day or permanently if necessary.

Poor Classroom Management Techniques Include:

- ✓ Yelling at children
- ✓ Constant threats to go to the director's office
- ✓ Being too much of a "buddy" with the children
- ✓ Any form of physical punishment
- ✓ Any punishment associated with food, toileting, or naps

The lists of violations regarding inappropriate punishment are almost endless and it is hard to imagine that anyone considered these things acceptable. Use the public information to do your own such research into inappropriate discipline. It can be unbelievable and even hard to read. Just a few examples taken from state citations over the years include:

❖ Lesson From the Field: Some Citations for Inappropriate Discipline

- ✓ *One particular center was cited for unusual and inappropriate punishment because they made the school-age children run for being too loud.*
- ✓ *Another center was cited in an incident for sprinkling water in children's faces and calling it "baptism" as their form of punishment.*
- ✓ *A center was cited for pulling and folding children's ears while forcefully placing their heads on mats at naptime.*
- ✓ *A center was cited for not demonstrating competency, good judgment, and self-control as they disciplined 3 to 4 years olds by pulling them by their hair; placing the children in a "monster room;" turning off the lights; and closing the door.*

Teaching Skills

This concept could warrant an entire book. We will touch briefly on the components of teaching skills here. Based on your center's design, curriculum, and goals research the best teaching methods and spend time teaching your staff how to develop and utilize these skills. Provide specific training on methods and curriculum for your teachers.

New teachers should have hands-on training under the supervision of one or more of your very best teachers. Have the supervising teachers explain what they do and why they do it throughout the process. This training can last days or even weeks. Be sure to have the supervising teachers elaborate on not only "why" things are done but specify which things are policies of the center and which things are dictated by licensing. Make sure that your new employee has a comprehensive understanding of both your center's policies for operations and your states regulations which are part of routine daily activities.

Use this comprehensive form of training for all new staff members even if they have experience in a licensed childcare operation and even if that experience is acceptable under your state standards. The fact that someone worked in a licensed center does not guarantee that they are fully competent in the area of childcare or that they know the regulations they are required to work within. Many operations do not operate by state standards, do not train their employees on the regulations, and operate facilities that are not always safe places for children.

It is your responsibility to uphold all of the highest standards in your center. This includes making sure that everyone is fully and completely trained prior to taking on the important responsibility of overseeing children. During interviews with candidates who had experience in licensed facilities, I found that many had little knowledge of the regulations. Some of these routinely left rooms of children unattended, didn't know required ratios, and weren't familiar with daily routine requirements for the children in care.

Investing in seminars can also be a wonderful way to provide such skills to your teachers. Choose seminars that will teach the skills and curriculum elements that will benefit your center as a whole. It can be expensive as you invest in seminar costs, transportation costs, and what is often over-time pay to send teachers to weekend training. Well chosen seminars will provide great benefits as your teachers return to the classroom with enthusiasm and new ideas to implement for the benefit of the children.

Be sure to document all training. This documentation includes both the study training as well as the time spent training under a lead teacher. Keep track of all the hours, all the areas covered, and include this in the personnel file. State childcare regulations will dictate the total number of hours required for training new teachers. Make sure all of the hours and areas are completely covered according to regulations. You may find that your staff needs even more training in particular areas in order to establish full competence prior to being allowed to be in charge of a class of children.

Liability Issues and Teachers

Teachers have to realize that the concept of liability reaches far beyond the possibility of the center being sued. The teachers in early childhood centers can be held personally liable if they are negligent in their care of children. It is important to make this a clear part of your training procedures to protect the children, the center, and the teachers who work for you. Your new staff members need to understand the extreme importance of this position and that they can be held personally liable for not carrying out the duties according to center policies and state regulations. Many teachers do not realize that not only can the center be held liable for the actions of the employee, but the employee herself can be sued and held personally liable for mistakes that may cause harm to children.

Another important inclusion in the area of study training is that of confidentiality. Teachers must realize that what goes on with children is not to be shared outside of the center with anyone. There are both ethical and legal issues inherent in dealing with children and they have rights to confidentiality.

Policy Meetings to Update and Remind

The reality is that scheduling meetings can be difficult as these generally have to be held outside of the work day. Unlike many workplaces where meetings are held within the schedule of the regular work day, all of the children are in care during all of those hours. Meetings usually mean adding more time to an already long work week. Even with that recognition, it is necessary to have periodic meetings to keep everyone "on the same page."

Even after your initial training, it is important to periodically have meetings where you discuss the policies. This allows you to remind staff of the policies they seem to be forgetting and also to update policies as needed. Employees who have been there for some time may forget about some policies that haven't been at the forefront in some time. Different situations over time can influence your policies and they will need updating and adapting from time to time.

Meetings should be completed before each new school term including both a new school year and summer. These meetings allow you to set the stage for the new term and get everyone on board. It is also a good time for teachers to re-organize, obtain new rosters, assess curriculum, clean, and re-organize rooms as they adjust for a change in the program. Other meetings should be held throughout the year as needed.

13

Staff Supervision

In this chapter, you will learn the key components of effective staff supervision including:

- Supervision Overview
- Hands-On Supervision
- Coordinating Different Personalities
- Coordinating Staffing Schedules
- Routine Supervision Practices
- Evaluations and Professional Development
- Using Monitoring Cameras
- Connecting With Your Staff

Supervision Overview

Staff supervision is a large part of managing a quality center. As the owner or director, you are directly responsible for everything that goes on inside the center. It is your job to maintain the safety of all of the children and make sure that all of the daily operations are run according to your state licensing standards. That means that you are responsible for the actions of all of your staff. The larger the staff and the bigger the center, the more complex this supervision becomes.

When a teacher inside a classroom makes a poor decision, a number of things can result. If a parent is angry, he may call you or a worst case scenario is that he may choose to call the state to report the situation creating a state investigation into your program. It isn't the teacher who will receive the citation from the state. It is the center. In some extreme cases, the state may cite the director if it is believed that she is not fulfilling her responsibility in managing a center according to state regulations.

Hands-On Supervision

All of the events going on in the classroom are your responsibility. This is why the hiring, training, and even releasing teachers from duty are such important parts of managing a quality operation. Those teachers that you place in the classroom must provide well for the children while following your operational policies and meeting all of the state mandated regulations.

Being a teacher in a classroom is a very challenging job. After hiring and training good teachers, you must provide the necessary support for those teachers. Children can be difficult to work with at times. Their parents can be equally difficult and unreasonably demanding at times. As the supervisor, you need to support the teachers who are doing a great job in your classrooms. Correct and assist the ones who are not. You need to be accessible and open to answer questions in order to help with the needs of those teachers.

Just search any state childcare citation site to find numerous violations based on the use of prohibited punishments and negligent supervision. Bad judgment by just one staff member can result in citations, investigations, injuries, and lawsuits.

Some violations sound almost unbelievable as there are citations for:

- ✓ Poking children with tacks
- ✓ Pinching
- ✓ Spanking
- ✓ Locking children in dark closets
- ✓ Walking out of a room and leaving a class of children unattended
- ✓ Leaving a child forgotten in a classroom
- ✓ Yelling at children
- ✓ Carrying out cell phone calls or texting while on duty
- ✓ Reading or doing other activities while in charge of a classroom
- ✓ Allowing children to run out of control in the classroom

The director is ultimately responsible for the behavior of every staff member. This means that it is absolutely imperative to be on site most of the time, know your staff, and be routinely present throughout the building … not stuck in the office with the pile of papers on your desk. This can be quite challenging at times as the regulatory and business paperwork can be a full time job in itself.

❖ Lesson From the Field: Bad Choices

> *One of the best examples of a lack of good judgment was a state citation. In the center, a child had managed to access a bottle of white correction fluid. The child painted the correction fluid over his body. The teacher tried to get it off and couldn't so she resorted to scrubbing it off with a "magic eraser" cleaning product. The rubbing of the cleaning product on the skin created abrasive burns on the child. This one was reported to the state based on the child's injuries.*

Clearly the teacher made a bad decision and didn't use common sense. In this example, if the director had been accessible and the teacher felt comfortable asking, it is likely that it would have ended quite differently. In my center, I was always accessible. I was available to my staff literally 24 hours a day. I did get calls and text messages from late nights to early mornings but this allowed me to fully manage and support my staff. Accessibility keeps you in charge, even when you are not on site. They contacted me whether in the building or by phone for everything they questioned which allowed the big (and sometimes small) decisions to come from me. (My side note: a solution to the real world lesson above: I could have told them that baby oil would have easily released the correction fluid from the skin – just as you would take off one of those temporary children's tattoos.) Having a director who is accessible and willing to help makes better solutions in almost all cases. Solutions that aren't obvious to younger or less experienced teachers in the classroom can be easily accessed by an experienced manager. There isn't a good substitute for knowledge based experience.

Coordinating Different Personalities

Disagreements and personality conflicts are also a part of personnel management. It is often necessary to take complaints and then further research exactly what those mean. Always keep in mind the complaint is coming from one person's perspective and is often only one piece of the entire situation. If you have one particular staff member who always seems to have problems with many other staff members, it may be time to look at the discussed concepts of "helping her decide to leave."

- ❖ Lesson From the Field: "What Do I Get?"

    When I rearranged the schedule to allow someone who works overtime on a regular basis to go home a couple of hours early, two teachers who had to take a different lunch time responded with: "What do I get out of it?" The reality that changes are made for the good of everyone on staff and the beneficiary varies during any one incident isn't obvious to many employees unless they are in direct benefit of the change in the particular situation. This had to be explained to them.

Another such example is evident in the following discussion from my center.

- ❖ Lesson From the Field: "As I See It..."

    Ms. Canton (one of the teachers) told our assistant director that she could not accommodate additional hours to help out if she was not given 24 hours prior notice. Two days later, she gave us 20 minutes notice that her child was sick and she would not come in that day.

Don't we all wish we could schedule our emergencies 24 hours in advance? In this world, schedule changes can happen in a very short time frame ... such as a teacher is called from a school to come get her own sick child. Another example would be when a teacher tries to work but is too sick and has to go home. Emergencies and illnesses happen and not on a predetermined schedule. Staff flexibility, regarding schedule changes, is very important. Make sure your teachers understand that even though they have to cover emergencies, no doubt there will be a time when someone will have to cover for their emergencies. This isn't a pile of paperwork and phone calls that can be taken care of on a different day. The children must be cared for by the correct number of teachers regardless of personal emergencies.

Be aware that you may have certain staff members who act very differently toward you than they do toward the other members of your team. These individuals may be very polite and professional to you and yet cause conflict within the total environment. Keep your eyes and ears open. Pay attention because these details can be easily overlooked while they create problems among your staff.

- ❖ Lesson From the Field: Keep Your Eyes Open

    One such example was an employee that I believed was very nice, polite, and a hard worker. Yet, when she wasn't in front of me she spread false statements including statements that I didn't like particular teachers, didn't trust them, and even told other staff members that I was going to fire them. In addition, the same trusted person would "snoop" through information in my office in order to appear to have more knowledge.

Just remember that "what you see is not always what you get" with people. Be diligent in supervision and have good communication with all of your employees. Information needs to be investigated. The reported situations are often true "through the eyes" of the person telling the story; however, these are not necessarily accurate accounts of the situation.

Coordinating Staffing Schedules

As the director, it is your job to carefully layout the staffing schedule. Many factors go into the layout of the schedule. The reality is, it isn't possible for the director to be on site every minute of every day that the center is open. Selecting who will manage all of the details when you are away is a very important decision. Even in a staff of many good teachers, there will probably only be a few that you want in that position. These will be the staff members that you want to have opening your center and closing your center at the end of the day, as well as managing in the director's absence.

Many good teachers are still not able to handle the additional challenges of managing. This person or few people need to be able to manage the center according to all of your policies and all of the state's regulations. They should be respected by the other employees and must be able to manage employees as needed. Other things that they will need to be able to handle include: parent concerns, children's emergencies, and managing an inspection should a state inspector show up.

The next step would be to determine how many staff members you need at each hour of the day. Determine the number you need based on how many children are expected to be at the center during each hour. An example would be opening with only two teachers; adding a third teacher thirty minutes later; and the other teachers arrive before your morning classes begin.

Always make sure that you have enough teachers to meet the state's required ratio. You absolutely need at least one more than is required. If you don't allow for this, then you will be out of ratio each time a teacher needs to use the restroom. The reality is that in order to always meet the state ratio; you need at least one additional staff member on duty. In very small centers, this can be the director. More ideally, this requires another teacher. If it fits your budget, consider hiring a floater, who can work in different rooms as needed and provide breaks for the teachers.

In a good program, with low student to teacher ratios, the number of teachers needed will be even higher. You determine the right number for your programs based on the number of children enrolled and the tuition charged to support the program. High quality and well staffed programs cost more to run. If you are providing these lower ratios, make sure that you let parents know this. Don't apologize for charging more simply let them know what they are getting for their money.

As you evaluate and staff for how many teachers your program needs, also make sure that you have created back up plans for extreme situations. Teachers do call in at the last minute due to their illnesses or their own children's illnesses. Other emergencies happen as well and you need to be prepared. This is when you really need the additional staff members. It is always a balancing game because a huge percentage of the cost of operating a childcare center is payroll. This means that you need to be staffed to an appropriate degree so that you can handle such situations. This staffing must be balanced with the cost of having those additional teachers on the regular schedule. Plans should be in place that allow you to have someone you can call in to work if necessary. This person can be a part-time employee, a trained substitute, or a temporary caregiver from a company who provides trained substitutes for childcare.

Even with the best of planning there will be rare instances that will truly test the ability to staff correctly. One of the most common of such occurrences is when the dreaded stomach virus hits. There can be some viruses which appear to be extremely contagious even when you are trying to send children home when ill; prevent children from coming to the center ill; along with cleaning and sanitizing the materials daily to stop the spread of the virus. Such situations happen. It can be very trying when teachers as well as students become very ill. You may find yourself with staffing shortages beyond what you were able to prepare for. This is where some of your best teachers will really shine. Have them work overtime as needed and reward their efforts with words of thank you, overtime pay, and bonuses as appropriate.

Staff scheduling goes far beyond having the right number of teachers. Make sure that you have a balanced staff at all times. This means that having enough people isn't all that is needed. You must balance those who are the most experienced with those who have less experience so that you are not leaving all of the inexperienced staff together at any particular time of day.

Routine Supervision Practices

Routine practices should include walking through the building and checking on teachers and their classes multiple times each day. The only way to really know what is going on is to be physically present. It lets the teachers know that you are aware of their classrooms and their work It also allows them access to you to ask questions and clarify details. This is your opportunity to check in and really know how the teachers are doing in their classrooms; how well they are managing the behavior; the quality of lessons; and ensure they are following the required procedures (such as documenting diaper changes and hand washing). Look around and check for any safety hazards such as uncovered electric outlets and tripping hazards on the floor. Work to educate teachers on safety practices and also insure that all procedures are followed.

It is your responsibility to make sure every teacher is following both state regulations and all of your procedures which go over and above those regulations. Ultimately, the safety and care of the children is your responsibility. Make sure that every classroom is a good place for children. This is also your opportunity to make sure that each teacher knows how many children are in her classroom and that all of the children are appropriately signed in on her roll sheet. Children may come and go at different times of the day and one may be in the restroom. Each teacher must know how many children she is responsible for and the location of every child in her care.

Evaluations and Professional Development

Early childhood teachers deserve to be treated as professionals who are respected and their talents valued. There is no more important job than making a difference in the lives of small children. For my center, I created an evaluation system to support professionalism. It set specific time frames for reviews, specific criteria for evaluations, and performance based pay increases as warranted.

Teachers should not be on a single rate of pay forever if they are doing a great job and are a true value to the organization. Likewise, they shouldn't have to come and ask for a raise. A more equitable system should be in place which rewards those who deserve it and assists those who are lower performers to enhance their skills.

Not all teachers will prove themselves on such a system, but it will create an equitable system which rewards high performers and helps you retain valuable workers. At a specified time on your system, take the time to meet with the teacher, and provide a written performance appraisal. This is the time to say how many wonderful things she is doing and also where she needs to improve. This allows true "professional development" through guiding teachers into being their very best in this field.

All that documentation that you were writing down as part of your staff supervision is very important in creating an accurate performance appraisal. You now have in your hands information on all of the great accomplishments the staff member made during the year. You also have verification of every time the person called in during the year; times when she didn't perform as desired, and other documented performance concerns. Hopefully there are more on the accomplishments list than on the problem list. Either way, you have pertinent information to create an accurate review. Being specific allows the employee to really see how her performance has "stacked up" during that period of time. She probably doesn't realize she called in ten times … it didn't seem like that much to her.

Pay increases are earned. Don't provide a pay increase for an under performer that you aren't even sure you want to keep. There should be distinct differences in pay between those you really need and count on and those you could easily replace. This is a valuable concept to make clear for all of your staff. Those who are great performers know that they are valued, counted on, and that they make considerably more money than others. This is very important when they wind up working extra hours because the lower end performers won't arrive early, stay late, or work through lunch on a tough day. In addition, it provides incentive for those who do want to progress to work harder and emulate those who are valuable employees.

I often used the phrase "who pulls the most weight." Other staff members know who works hard and who doesn't. Let new employees know that you have a hard working staff and if they don't jump in and do their share, the experienced staff will notice and you will as well.

Keep in mind that your higher performers should also be in training to take on more responsibility as it is needed. Clearly, advancement depends on this. It is wonderful to have a great classroom teacher. Those who advance to help oversee the center have to be able to see even more. They need to have a level of dedication to the center as a whole and every detail … including those well past teaching in a classroom. These staff members understand the concepts of: meeting every licensing standard; supervising other employees; being responsible for purchasing food and supplies; and helping to oversee all details of the center, not just their classroom and not just during business hours.

As you do choose to give staff members greater responsibility and move them into managerial positions. Make it evident. Provide notice to your entire staff that you are giving them extra responsibility and that you expect the other team members to respect their new role. It can be very difficult for team member to progress from being a part of the team, to being in a supervisory position over others.

Using Monitoring Cameras

Cameras are not a substitute for being physically present in the classrooms; however, if you choose to have them in your center, these can be useful for monitoring classrooms as a secondary method of safety. Cameras are widely used and can be a good source for increasing the knowledge of what is going on inside classrooms and ultimately the safety of the children in care. If you decide to use cameras you can choose whether these are recorded or not. If you are recording the classrooms, make sure that your employees are aware of this. It is a good idea to get this acknowledgement in writing.

Cameras can be used as a monitoring devise for the management of the center without using a recording device. They can also be used for recording and even be designed where parents can view the children from the internet. Be aware that those recordings and internet viewings can be used against you if a parent sees something that she doesn't like. It is also important to note that the little piece that the parent sees may not present a clear picture of what was occurring at the time. In addition, it opens up the scrutiny of information and pictures of other people's children to all parents who are viewing. Also be aware that, if you are recording the events, these tapes may be taken by the state regulatory agency for review if they desire to use them, particularly during an investigation.

❖ Lesson From the Field: Monitoring with Cameras

A parent who was interested in our preschool had come to sit in on the preschool room activities. Ms. Anton was in charge of the room because the lead teacher had just left employment with us that week. We had a new person in training also in the room. I looked on the monitors to find the children being wild and running all over the room. I looked at the experienced teacher in my office and said: "Can you fix it?" She walked in and almost instantly had the room back in order with the children behaving well. She also took time to talk to the parent, explain that we had someone leave recently, and someone in training. This was not the normal way we operated. The parent signed the enrollment forms and the child joined our program.

There are both positive aspects to using cameras and negative case scenarios for such usage. Research all of the issues including those of ethical concerns, state regulations, and legal issues which may surround the use of cameras. Then make an informed decision as to whether you will use cameras. If you decide to use the cameras, then take a careful look at all the issues when deciding how you will use the cameras.

Considerations to evaluate regarding the use of monitoring cameras:

- ✓ Determine where the monitors will be displayed.
- ✓ Determine who will be allowed to view them.
- ✓ Decide if you will use them as an internal monitoring device only, or will you make them accessible to parents over the internet?
- ✓ If you are recording, will you keep the tapes or record over them daily?
- ✓ If you retain the recordings, how long will they remain on file?

Carefully consider which method and system you will use. There isn't a right or wrong answer, but there are many aspects which should be considered in determining what is right for your center.

Connecting With Your Staff

Make an effort to connect with your staff members. Support them in their work, and strive to provide a good work atmosphere. Many management books explore the concepts of the importance to staff of a good relationship with their supervisor. It works to create a good team when there is a positive atmosphere along with a good relationship between the director and the caregivers. Most of your employees will work harder and put more effort into their job if they feel that they are respected, supported, and have a good relationship with you. This is very important as a means for increasing job satisfaction in a highly stressful field. It has the potential to reduce turnover and reduce absenteeism. It also increases the willingness of employees to fill in when you are short staffed.

It is a good idea to substitute for short periods in different classrooms from time to time. This allows you to stay connected to what it is really like inside the classroom. It keeps you in tune with all the daily challenges that are a part of the early childhood classroom. As a good director, this helps keep the right perspective and balance between what you need from a business standpoint and what is needed inside the classroom. Make sure that the ratios and the particular children within each classroom create a situation which can be appropriately managed. Just because the state allows a particular number, doesn't mean that you have to put that many children in a classroom. Keep in mind that the number of children in a classroom may need to vary at times. Some students "count as more than one" due to the increased teachers efforts that it can take to manage particular children with more challenging behaviors. Taking a little time to "work" inside the classroom keeps these managerial aspects aligned with the realities.

With all this being said make sure that the relationship is positive and supportive but also make sure that it remains professional. It is important to show that you care about personal concerns and do what you can as a supervisor to assist; however, it equally important to not be personally involved with your staff members. You are still the supervisor and must remain in a position which is respected allowing you to appropriately manage your staff. Take care of your staff and you will find some very valuable employees who will take care of you. I often used the statement we would "make it work." That usually meant managing with a short staff, I loved it when I got that statement back on occasion as my best teachers would tell me they would "make it work" when I needed to be out.

14

Staff Health and Safety

In this chapter, you will learn the importance of staff safety and how to implement safety policies and procedures including:

- Staff Safety Overview
- Health Practices
- Staff and Illnesses
- Insurance to Protect Staff
- Troubling Incidences on the Job

Staff Safety Overview

The safety of your staff members is another important part of the vast managerial components of operating a high quality center. You need to put into place policies and procedures that not only take care of the children but that will also take care of your staff. You do this by making their workplace safe and protecting them from injuries and potential hazards.

Health Practices

Health procedures need to be in place and adhered to on a regular basis. These include basic concepts like always having plastic gloves readily available for teachers to use when handling situations involving children's bodily fluids such as fecal matter and blood. These are hazards that your staff will come into contact with routinely. Diaper changes of bowel movements should require caregivers to wear gloves. Children have accidents resulting in bleeding; potty accidents; feces on the floor or other objects; and they contract illnesses which result in diarrhea and vomiting. All of these situations should mandate the use of plastic gloves and careful sanitation practices while taking care of children. Have gloves available for teachers outside as well. They can carry a first aid kit including gloves with them. If a child is injured on the playground and bleeds profusely, they need gloves right then. There isn't time to go inside and get some before helping the child.

Create a policy for how your staff members will handle blood soaked clothing and feces covered clothing. Will they be required to wash it out? Will they throw it away? Will they bag it up and send it home for the parents to clean? This is an area that can become quite controversial to parents as there are so many different ideas of how your "should" handle such situations.

As with other situations that can have numerous "right" answers, think it through, create a policy that is best for your center. Write it down. Train your staff on how to handle the situation and then be ready to stand by that decision when parents question it. It is your policy and this is why. Don't waiver or change under pressure. Make an informed decision and a policy that is justified, and then stick with it.

Many times I had to defend this practice but I steadfastly held to my belief that cleaning soiled clothes was not part of our work. In addition, I wouldn't put feces, blood, or vomit soiled clothing or towels into our washers as I focused on overall sanitation within the center.

❖ Lesson from the Field: A Bag of Poop

> *On one such occasion, a parent got very angry because she was sent home with what she called "a bag of poop." Clearly it wasn't that bad but she did receive a bag of soiled clothing that she didn't want to clean. (Which in my opinion was fine ... she could throw it away.) What she wanted was for the teachers to have cleaned it. Her little boy was working on potty training at school but she didn't want to do it at home because it was messy. She suggested someone at least take the clothes out and hose them off. I answered with: "Have you ever hosed anything off outside?" The teachers were likely to be wearing the feces by the time they got through "hosing" the clothes off.*
>
> *Based on the fact that she was not willing to clean her own child's clothes and unwilling to work on potty training at home, I told her we would put a diaper on her child and no longer do potty training with him. The next week, I received a note of apology and a request to continue potty training along with the statement that she would work on the training at home. All was forgiven and we went back to potty training.*

Staff and Illnesses

Also be aware of illnesses and diseases which can be transmitted to the teachers at your center. Usually the first year or two is the hardest with respect to contracting illnesses for individuals who have not worked with small children. Over time, most individuals will develop strong immune systems and not get sick very often, even when working right in the middle of young children who readily share their germs.

Even the most experienced teachers will still find that they become ill at times, when certain highly contagious diseases make their way through your center (such as the stomach viruses and pneumonia). Respect the fact that teachers are ill and do need to recover. It is difficult to work with a less than full staff, but requiring teachers to be at work when they are sick and contagious can mean that those illnesses continue to stay at the center and spread. Just as children are sent home when they are sick, allow those teachers who are ill to go home.

Also be aware of safety when it comes to teachers who are pregnant or have other health concerns. There are some childhood diseases, which are not seen as much of a hazard to healthy adults, but that can be hazardous to an unborn child. Along the same line, make sure that you adjust the work load as needed for teachers who are pregnant or recuperating from physical problems. Create an environment and a system which cares about your staff and supports good health and safety.

Insurance to Protect Staff

As another support for employees, be aware that your liability insurance may not cover your employees if they are hurt on the job. For both their protection and the financial protection of your business, make sure that you have a form of insurance to protect your employees while on the job.

The following are just a few examples of on the job injuries:

- ✓ Kitchen cutting injuries
- ✓ Kitchen burn injuries
- ✓ Slips and falls
- ✓ Injuries obtained from handling out of control children

Troubling Incidences on the Job

Another job difficulty for teachers is that of angry and unpredictable parents. Try to make sure that you have taken care of situations which will put your staff in a difficult position. Call parents prior to pick up if you feel they will have an extreme reaction to a particular circumstance (injuries, actions by other children, etc). Take time on the phone with them and make sure they have come to terms with it prior to leaving for the day. If you feel a situation may continue to escalate when the parent arrives, then don't leave until the parent has come and picked up the child. Be there, be available, and take care of the very difficult situations where parents may act inappropriately with your staff. This is discussed in detail in Chapter 17: Parents' Behaviors.

A less common situation, but one that you very well may see if you spend years in the business is that of teachers collapsing at work. For different reasons, a teacher may become very ill at work. Teachers may be in a classroom with children when they become ill. Make sure that your teachers are not isolated from others, so that they can reach someone if they need to do so. In addition, you need emergency contact information for all of your employees so that if an emergency happens, you can contact someone for them. It can also involve calling 911 and having an ambulance come to assist the teacher.

15

Teachers and Their Own Children

In this chapter, you will explore a situation that is rare in most other fields: The concept of employees bringing their own children to work with them on a daily basis. You will learn the benefits and challenges to such a practice including:

- The Unique Situation
- Benefits
- Complications
- Weighing the Benefits and Complexities
- Complications can Extend to Family Members

The Unique Situation

Childcare is one of the few fields where employees not only request but often expect to be allowed to bring their children to work with them. It creates a very unique situation which can provide both benefits and great complications within the center. It is very common for job applicants calling about an advertised position to ask outright if they can bring their children for free.

Different centers have varying policies in this area. It is a concept that deserves careful consideration and consistent implementation. Whatever policies are determined must be implemented fairly and consistently for all staff members. As you create policies, keep in mind that some decisions may have to be made based on enrollment. Will you have the capacity (based on your stated license capacity) for the employees' children? Also, fully assess the cost of providing care for these children. If you are not at full capacity, the cost of keeping staff members' children without charging them will include: supplies used, food, and the payroll cost of supervising those additional children. If you are at capacity, the staff members' children are taking the place of children who would be paying full tuition and then the real cost becomes much higher.

Some centers do not allow employees to bring their children unless they pay the full tuition. Other centers allow their teachers to bring one child at no cost or a reduced cost but pay full tuition for other children. Still others even allow teachers to bring multiple children without any charges.

Benefits

Why would you even consider giving away free childcare or a reduced tuition for employees? Why would you let valuable enrollment spaces be taken with children who are not paying the full rate? There are many women and men who have children and are not able to make enough to pay for childcare. This means that having a job which allows them to obtain an income and not have to pay the full tuition can be a huge benefit. There are many good candidates for jobs in childcare centers who would not be able to work there if they were charged the full rate. By allowing parents to bring their children with them at a free or reduced rate, as a part of working at your center, you can employ wonderful individuals who stay with you for years. They are not only good early childhood teachers, but they have the benefit of bringing their children to work with them.

If you do allow employees to bring their children to work with them be sure to make your policies clear and in compliance with all applicable employment laws. Also establish where you draw the line? Will you allow the grandmother to bring her grandchildren, that are living with her, to the center at the same discounted rate? What about aunts and uncles? It is a good idea to consult legal advice to make sure your policy choices are within legal guidelines. In addition, you should consult your CPA regarding any tax ramifications on this benefit, just as you would for all other benefits provided to your employees.

Complications

The negative aspects of allowing staff members to bring their children to work with them center on the same difficulties that you have with many other parents. There is nothing that brings out the overreaction and the emotional side of people more than issues surrounding their children. It is a natural response. Parents care deeply about their children and want to provide the best they can for their children. They want to protect them from anything hurtful and they see everything through eyes that are focused on their own children (rather than the procedures that focus on what is best for all of the children).

This emotional response to their own child or children's needs creates numerous complexities within the center. These staff members may break rules when it comes to their own children; they may not like how other teachers handle their children; and they become upset when their children are sad or have to have a consequence. Even teachers who are good at classroom management are often not able to handle their own child's behaviors. Children react differently to correction by a parent than they do to other teachers.

Some teachers are very accepting, appreciative, and even encourage other teachers to help with their child's behavior. Others become offended and take issue with the situation. These realities leave the director in the position of maintaining a balance of dealing with issues based on staff members concerns for their own children. These personal situations leave directors with more internal complications than would face managers in most other industries.

When teachers are unhappy with respect to their own children in the center, they are quick to forget that they are receiving a huge benefit. Don't be surprised when they don't appreciate the efforts that have been extended to them and blame you for all of the things that they consider not right for their own child.

It is preferable for the staff members' children to be assigned to the classrooms of other teachers. The reality is that in small centers, this is not always possible. Children may have to be in the classroom with their parent as the teacher. This is always a challenging situation, but for many parents it can work just fine. For other parents, it is absolutely not possible to work with their own child in a classroom. It is always more complicated to manage your own child's behaviors and some teachers can't do it.

Weighing the Benefits and Complexities

Balance the issues with the benefits. For some staff members, bringing their child to work is a huge benefit. These employees will understand the value of what they are getting. Policies which support the parents who work for you can also provide you with wonderful employees. These teachers will often stay with you for a long time as they are able to recognize the benefits that this brings to them both as a parent and from a financial standpoint.

Very caring parents usually make very caring teachers for the children in your center. Having this understanding, of how parents feel, helps teachers to be more sensitive to the needs of the parents of children in care. However, it is important to point out to these parents that the job is about caring for other people's children. The benefits of bringing their child to work are clear, but while at work it is about the care, education, and support of all of the children.

All of these realities should be included in the analysis of your policies regarding employees bringing their children to the center with them. As in all decisions, make your policies carefully. Follow through with and enforce your policies. Nothing happens in a vacuum. If you deviate from those policies, be ready to do it for everyone. Remember that what you do, even for what seems like one time, sets a precedent. If you do something for one staff member or one child, you will be expected to do it for all of them. Policies which are not consistently enforced are no longer real policies.

Complications can Extend to Family Members

The same type of complexities can occur when you have nieces, nephews, close friends' children, and even grandchildren of employees in care. The situation initiates from the same cause, a very close "parental type" connection to these children that skews the view of how a teacher relates to these children.

❖ Lesson From the Field: Family Members

I had an adorable little girl that was related to one of my teachers (but not her own child). The teacher was over protective of the child and saw things surrounding this child through that distorted vision. When the child was moved into another teacher's classroom, problems escalated. The teacher began to say how bad the other classroom was. These issues were investigated and found to be unsubstantiated. In addition, the child's mother had issues with the child not being in the family member's classroom anymore. Under those conditions, the best remedy was to move her back into the classroom the teacher and parent preferred.

Is it worth it? Do the benefits outweigh the inherent problems of employees bringing their children to work with them? That is for you to determine. The only note of caution is: Adding a benefit is easy; however, it is very difficult to take away the benefit later.

16

Children's Behaviors

In this chapter, you will explore the scope of children's behaviors from learning good behavior to truly difficult behaviors including:

- Overview of Children's Behaviors
- Teaching Appropriate Behavior
- Typical Children's Behaviors
- Discipline and the Director's Office
- Developmental Delays
- Extreme Children's Behaviors
- Dismissing Children From the Program

Overview of Children's Behaviors

There are many children who have very good behavior. These children are an absolute joy to work with in the center. The reality is that they don't need a chapter in a book. The challenges fall with those who have more difficult behaviors.

Consistency is one of the great keys to obtaining positive behaviors in young children. If the rules are explained and then implemented every day by every teacher, it becomes understood and routine. Young children are comfortable and understand such routines. They know exactly what to expect each day. Set the rules and expectations for both parents and children. For example, if the children are not to bring toys with them, make it clear. Then when they arrive and they are carrying a toy, meet them at the door and send it back home with the parent. You have reinforced the rule for both the child and the parent. Just as in other situations, rules that are not enforced consistently are not really rules or policies at all. In addition, if one child is allowed to have the rule "bent" then others are justified in expecting the same privilege.

Even with this enforcement and understanding, you will still encounter parents who simply won't deal with the behavior or don't know how to control the child. These parents are leaving it up to you.

- ❖ Lesson From the Field: Enforcing the Rules

    One such example was a parent who allowed her child to wear little play shoes with high heels and no backs to school. We didn't allow that type of shoe due to the fact that they can easily contribute to falls in young children. She dropped the child off at the door and when we addressed the shoes issue, she said there was a change of shoes in the little girl's backpack. She turned to the child and said: "See, I told you they don't allow these at preschool" leaving the rule enforcement to the center.

- ❖ Lesson From the Field: Parent's Who Avoid Being the Disciplinarian

    Another such example was a child who was brought in daily with a toy, even though we didn't allow toys from home in the classroom. The little boy's mother would drop him off with the toy, knowing that the first thing the teacher had to do was take the toy away and the child would then go into screaming tantrums. Why would she do this? The tantrum was coming and she didn't want to deal with it. She left the discipline up to us.

This is one of the causes of why children misbehave. The rules in some homes are few if any. The children are allowed to do whatever they wish. Coming into a structured environment where good behavior is expected is quite a change from their home realities. There are numerous reasons for misbehavior in young children. This example is only one. Some behaviors are simply developmental. The children are still learning how to appropriately respond to things. Other children may have more complex issues influencing their behaviors.

Teaching Appropriate Behavior

Most children's behaviors are simply a learning process. Young children, and often their parents as well, need help in establishing how to achieve good behavior. For children who have more challenging behaviors (but not extreme and violent behaviors), it can be very beneficial to work with the parents on helping children to behave better. Numerous parents of children with challenging behaviors do not know how to work on these behaviors. Some will even tell you that they don't know what to do with the child.

Work with these parents to create cohesiveness between home and school. Behavior charts can be beneficial for communicating how well a child behaved during the day. This allows for a school to home connection with a behavior system. There are numerous ways to help parents work with their children to learn good behavior. Different systems may work better for different children. We are only going to discuss two basic strategies here which are: reward based systems and consequence based systems.

Parents may want to set up reward systems that include information provided from school in that system. Preferable reward systems are those which build but don't start over when a child makes a mistake. An example would be the use of stickers; after a child achieves enough stickers, she can have a reward. Rewards can be simple such as a little toy or a trip with a parent to have an ice cream cone. Essentially what you want to build on is the concept that a child has to think about the consequences, before choosing her actions. This takes some time and is a developmental process.

The opposite of reward systems are systems which have consequences. If the behaviors weren't appropriate, then the child loses a privilege or has something taken away. I strongly prefer a positive reward system rather than a consequence system. Reward systems which continue to build allow the child to achieve and feel the benefits. This ultimately should lead to repeating the positive actions and learning correct behaviors. Not everyone believes in reward systems. The system chosen should be based upon the foundation of the center's programs and the input from the parents.

Typical Children's Behaviors

It is necessary to manage many children, teach appropriate behaviors, correct inappropriate behaviors, and help children learn how to behave. Young children are learning. From a very early age they understand how to get their teachers attention and how to show that they aren't happy. Children have to learn how to express themselves appropriately and it is a natural part of the daily routine in a center.

Temper tantrums, pushing, biting, and scratching are all part of expressing how a child feels. These behaviors are fairly typical and teaching children to "use their words" rather than act out is a basic part of early childhood education. Usually teaching correct behavior revolves around simple correction, re-direction, or even a short period of sitting out of the activities. Over time most children will progress and behaviors will improve.

Toilet Training can be challenging for some children and for others it is almost uneventful. Many parents rush the toilet training which can create problems. Some children are successful with toilet training at a very young age even before two years old. Other children learn between two and three or even a little later. Usually when children are ready to be toilet trained they learn quickly. If they are rushed or pushed to start too young it can take months which can be frustrating for both the child and the grownups involved in the process.

If a child is interested in the "potty" and appears to be ready, then give it a try. If however after several days or a week, the child still doesn't seem to understand at all, then stop. Wait for awhile and try again rather than continuing to push and frustrate.

Many centers divide children by age but put an additional restriction on children who are not toilet trained. It is relatively common for childcare centers to not allow a child to move up with the next class until they are toilet trained. This is typically true of the "3 year old" class. Most programs, directors, and teachers assume that the child should be potty trained by three.

Potty training is part of your program if you enroll children as infants and toddlers. It is part of the growing and learning process. There are also numerous parents who want the center to potty train the child for them. They don't want to deal with the mess at home. It is generally not a method that will work. It is a method that often confuses children. When the parent arrives and puts on a diaper or pull up to go home, it means the child no longer has to go to the toilet. This culminates at the center into the fact that the children have more accidents because sometimes they are expected to go in the toilet and sometimes not. They don't necessarily remember when they have on the diaper or pull up and when they don't.

If it takes a little longer, for a child to become toilet trained, it should still not really be a concern. However if it extends well past three years old, it probably should be referred to the parents to have it evaluated related to potential developmental delays. These same children who seem to have more difficulties may also have unusual behaviors.

Toileting Behavior Concerns

- ✓ Going to the restroom and yet urinating and defecating on the floor rather than in the toilet
- ✓ Using toilet issues as a way of acting out such as intentionally urinating in the floor
- ✓ Urinating on the floor after just returning from the potty

Some of the actions may be deliberate and some of these actions may be more connected to developmental issues. I've watched numerous incidences under both conditions. Be aware of such things and watch for possible developmental concerns with children who have more trouble than usual and for much longer periods of time.

Biting is an extremely common, yet very frustrating, behavioral concern. Some children seem to just have a tendency to bite while others do not. Biting can occur at any age in early childhood but is very prevalent in the twelve months up to three year old age groups. Some children will bite as a response to anger. For example, a child bites another because the friend tried to take his toy. Another more extreme example is that of children who act out and bite anyone around them when they are angry. The victim in such cases just happened to be the person available for the child to take out his frustrations on. Other children will bite simply out of overstimulation, excitement, or other reasons. These children aren't angry, they just bite.

Handling biting is challenging, particularly because it seems to be largely a repeated offense. Be consistent. Correct the biter every time and comfort the victim of the offense. Explain that it hurts; try to teach the child to "think before he acts." This is a learning process and it takes time. Biting is largely instant and reactive. Teaching a child to remember there will be a consequence before taking action takes time. Over time consistency will work.

Should you withdraw a child from your program for biting? As with all policies, fully analyze all of your considerations. Withdrawing every small child who bites may make quite a negative impact on enrollment. Biting is hurtful but it is a common early childhood behavior. What will you do if one of your best teachers has a child who bites repeatedly? Will you make that child leave as well? Doing so will mostly likely leave you without one of your best teachers. Make a policy and then stick with it. Some centers withdraw children for biting and others do not.

Over the years, I chose to work with biters. It was difficult and frustrating at times but I watched the children with this behavior problem overcome it over time. I had the joy of seeing these children grow and develop into absolutely wonderful older children. Many stayed all the way through the school–age program. If I hadn't chosen to work with them, they would have simply moved on to someone else.

❖ Lesson From the Field: Biters

I told this story many times over the years as I dealt with angry phone calls from the parents of children who had been bitten at the center. My first experience with biting involved my own first child. He went to the toddler room at his childcare center and was routinely bitten. I found it frustrating and I certainly wasn't taking it in stride with his teachers. Then later, I got to feel the other side as my second child was the biter. I loved her center and I was really glad that they worked with my child rather than kicked her out for this behavior.

As with all other disciplinary issues, if it's not extreme, and not beyond what you are able to handle, then it is usually better to help the child learn and grow. It is all about making a real difference in the lives of children and their families.

Discipline and the Director's Office

When teachers can't control particular children and need them removed from the classroom, it seems they most often wind up in the director's office. Unless your program is large enough to support an extra person to handle such situations, this is likely the case. On one hand this system seems to make sense in that the director becomes the ultimate authority and should be able to manage the children that the teacher cannot. In addition, a single child can be very disruptive in the learning environment. That child needs to be removed from that setting for both the child's behavior correction as well as to maintain an appropriate learning environment for the other children.

The "other hand" involves the reality of managing the business end while there are misbehaving children (often multiple children) in the office at the same time. There were times when it seemed that having a child or two in my office screaming or throwing a temper tantrum was an almost daily event. At times it happened even multiple times throughout a single day. I would try to get the work done while surrounded by the loud piercing screams of the misbehaving children who had come to "sit in Dr. Busch's office." Handling business calls is not possible under such circumstances.

I sent notes home each time with information and expected the parents to talk to their children about appropriate behavior. It is important that discipline is shared between the parents and the center. This does improve overall discipline.

While sending children to the office can be an effective technique at times, it should not be over used. When used too often the teacher is clearly unable to manage her classroom, or is choosing not to work on the behaviors within the classroom. In these situations, the issue should be addressed directly with the teacher. Removing the child from the classroom and into the care of the director should be a last resort on a rare occasion … not the way to make her work easier.

Developmental Delays

Working with very young children provides the opportunity to help children and their parents by watching their developments over time. Some children will not appear to be achieving developmental milestones. Look at the research on milestones for particular age groups as well as keep notes of unexpected and on-going difficulties for these children. Be aware of the ranges of knowledge and skills for the various age groups of children in your care. When you see concerns in development, it is time to take further action to help children.

When you see that a child is not performing at the expected rate for his age, this information should be shared with his parents. Many parents do not see it. As expected, parents see what the child is learning and accomplishing rather than what he is not doing. This is especially true for newer parents who don't have other children to compare the development to. When delays are suspected, share the information with parents. Encourage parents to talk to their pediatrician and seek outside testing. For children with developmental delays, discovering this early can allow earlier intervention and potentially greater benefits for the child.

If children are sent on for further evaluations, it is typical for the doctor or other behavioral specialist to request information from the teacher. The teacher can provide enormous insight into the child's development since she works with him on a regular basis. This often comes in the form of a survey. Sometimes it will include a personal interview and at other times a specialist may come to the center to observe the child in the childcare environment. After complete assessment and diagnoses of a behavioral problem or delay is made for a child, the specialist should provide the center with information on what can be done to help him. Follow the instructions and provide the services as long as it is something that is feasible for the center.

Directors and teachers will see children with developmental delays, autism, and other special needs. For the most part, an early childhood program should be able to support these families by providing the best possible opportunities for these children. Opportunities include spending time working with them on their needs and carrying out special instructions from doctors or other specialists.

Even if the needs are developmental, if the needs are extreme and beyond what the center is able to manage then it is necessary to let the parent know that. If you can't support what the child needs, or the behaviors are extreme enough to pose hazards to the other children in care, you will have to withdraw the child from your program. Be supportive and understanding as you relay the information. As always, your focus must be on the benefits of a high quality program for all of the children.

Extreme Children's Behaviors

Extreme behaviors fall under a completely different category. These behaviors include violent behaviors which place other children and even staff members in harm's way. It is hard to believe that in early childhood, behaviors can be this extreme but it is a reality and it's not that unusual. Even children at this age can be extremely hard to control when they are very angry and in a violent state. In the moment, some children can actually be very strong and very hard to manage. Children in these situations can hit, kick, bite, throw furniture, and knock over chairs and shelving units in an attempt to destroy things. Sometimes these children will even run out of the room, through the building, or even out of the front door. It is these extreme behaviors which need to be seriously addressed as to the cause and the solution. Most childcare centers are not staffed or able to handle such extreme behaviors. These behaviors can harm other children and create situations where employees are injured in their attempts to manage the child.

There are a number of potential causes for extreme behaviors which include a lack of discipline, home environments, and true behavioral problems. It is very difficult to distinguish whether these behaviors are due to a lack of discipline in the child or diagnosable behavioral problems. To compound the issue, many pediatricians and other professionals who work with behavior problems will refuse to evaluate or diagnose such problems while the children are still in the preschool years. It appears that many professionals in this area have trouble distinguishing the difference as well. You will find that some parents are able to get a professional diagnoses and assistance for dealing with such behaviors while others are not able to find someone who will evaluate these behaviors. One additional problem with diagnosis is that at times parents may have to wait months or even over a year to get in to see a specialist for behavioral analysis.

The first step to managing a child who is having an extreme behavioral episode involves removing the child from the room with other children. This protects the other children in care, provides less audience for the episode, and also prevents other children from witnessing poor behaviors. These situations actually take three people to handle the incident caused by one child. One teacher remains with the class. The child has to be removed from all of the other children and the second teacher must stay with the child and try to manage the behavior. The third person must call and try to reach the parent because this situation demands that the child must leave the center and be placed back into the parent's care.

Even if it is clear that you are not able to manage the child's behavior, remember calling the parent to come and pick up the child is not a fast fix. It is still necessary to manage the child until the parent arrives. This can involve just having someone stay with and supervise the child while he continues the rage. If it's feasible, this is the best option. Sometimes the child will not allow this as he attempts to throw things, damage the facility, or run from the teacher. This may require the child to be held to keep from injuring himself or others. Keep in mind that even during the efforts to control him; you have to utilize "appropriate discipline" and great care.

Children who go into these rages will cause worry and concern for the director. It is very difficult to ever leave the building when you don't know when the child may go into a violent rage. It isn't right to expect your staff members to have to continually handle such behaviors and quite frankly even if they were willing; few have the ability to manage it.

The actual remedies that the center has are very limited. Appropriate discipline in childcare centers is limited to re-directing children, talking to them, having them sit out from the group and other such methods. The extreme remedies available in childcare include calling parents and even having them come and pick up their child. You may even find situations where the parents don't see these behaviors that you see and question you. The reality is this: If they are not requiring the child to do something, they may not see the extreme reactions. A lack of discipline at home can be contributing to the overall problem.

Dismissing Children from the Program

If a child repeatedly has such episodes, it is best to take measures to have the child dismissed from your program. It can't lead to anything good. If the child stays, you are impacting the program value and safety of all the other children on a regular basis. Childcare centers are group environments, if it takes one caregiver to watch over a child with extreme behaviors on a regular basis, then that child needs to be withdrawn from the program.

When there is a child in the center with these types of extreme behaviors, it is important to document each incident. Send a copy of the documentation home to the parent. Express your concern through these notes and phone calls to parents. Keep a copy of each documentation record in your confidential files. Documentation of these extreme behavioral occurrences should include the date, time, staff members involved, and specific behaviors of the child. This is important in an industry which carries a high degree of liability. Protect the children. Do what is right. Do what is necessary to protect the safety of the child with behavior problems and the other children around him. Document your occurrences and keep all of that documentation! Create a confidential file that is in a separate location from those files that are auditable. This is your file and your documentation. Unless you are required to keep such records by your state regulatory agency; it should not be included in your student files.

The parents must work with you to correct the behaviors if it is going to work. Ultimately they have the control over the child, the center does not. If they won't work with you and coordinate at home to teach the child good behavior, all of the efforts put in at school will probably not work. It is a team effort and must be addressed with the parents.

❖ Lesson From the Field: Parent's Who Can't Manage Their Young Children

I have told a number of parents who said they couldn't control their children: "He is only three. You can still pick him up and move him. What are you going to do when he is as big as or even bigger than you?" Good behavior along with respect for parents and authority starts early. Children who do not learn this in early childhood may have much bigger consequences as they get older.

When there is a pattern of extreme behaviors which take away from your focus of a quality center that benefits all of the children, then it becomes necessary to withdraw the child from your program. By the time the decision has been reached that you are not able to manage the behavioral needs of the child, it should not come as a surprise to the parents. Never start a conversation or behavior notice with: "It's been going on for some time…" or "This is the third time…" Keep the parents informed and bring them into the process of working to correct the behavior. They have much more flexibility in controlling their child's behavior than the staff at the center.

Requiring a child to withdraw can be the right thing. It can be very difficult; however, it doesn't change the fact that the situation is not working as a part of a good group environment for children. There were times when I really liked the parents and really sympathized with the situation that they were not able to control but the reality didn't change. We were not able to accommodate this child who exhibited behaviors that we could not improve or control.

Remember even through the frustrations and documentation of such events, you are required to provide confidentiality for that child and his parents. This is not information that you are at liberty to talk about with others or share. Do not discuss incidents with any outside people or parents, other than the parents of that particular child. If another child was hurt or affected during the incident, then their parent should be advised of what happened to their child … but do not provide the name of the child who committed the offenses to the other child's parents. The great irony here is that the children know who did it and they will tell their parents; however, as a matter of professionalism and confidentiality, the center's representatives may not share the name of the child committing offenses to anyone else.

17

Parents' Behaviors

In this chapter, you will examine the impact of parents' behaviors on your center including:

- Overview of Parent Interactions
- When Parents Have Difficult Behaviors
- Handling Phone Calls From Angry Parents
- Choose Friends Carefully
- Making Tough Choices

Overview of Parent Interactions

In childcare, you have the pleasure of working with many wonderful parents. There are many people that you truly enjoy conversing with and even some that become life-long friends. You truly value those parents who work within your policies and structures; communicate concerns with you in an appropriate conversation; and generally work with you to create that very valuable home-school connection.

For almost all parents, grandparents, and guardians, their children are the absolute most important people in their lives. Nothing brings out the emotional side of people more than their children. Establishing a good relationship with parents is the first step in working with them. Be available often. This means that the director should be regularly at the center when parents are there. A good schedule can include being on site to close a couple of nights a week. Being available at the beginning of the day is also good; however, the end of the day is a preferable time for availability and communicating with parents. This is due to the fact that most parents will be in a hurry trying to drop of children and get to work on time in the morning. While making yourself available, try to not only be on site but be out front and easily accessible.

Directors will learn more and be more in touch if they are easily accessible. Parents will chat about things their children learned, express what they are happy about, as well as share little concerns. They will readily do this when the director is friendly and available. Many parents are less likely to seek you out for these types of communications. Easily accessible, means that parents remain happy, issues are dealt with while they are small, and the director is in touch with the concerns of parents.

When Parents Have Difficult Behaviors

While listening to parents, and taking care of those "little details" as they arise, the management staff is largely able to avoid big problems. Most big problems stem from little things that haven't been addressed and these issues grow into bigger problems with angry and frustrated parents.

Some challenging parent behaviors I experienced included:

- ✓ Anger because a child didn't have insect repellent put on every time he went outside whether there were mosquitoes present or not
- ✓ Anger over not feeding a child junk food which was in her lunch sent from home
- ✓ Slamming doors and walking out because a child was scratched by another child
- ✓ A parent who told her child there was a big new slide on the playground (there wasn't) to get her child to go to school
- ✓ Dropping a child off and telling the child that if he had a potty accident the teacher would call the police to come and get him

Another common concern is that of being placed "in the middle" of family issues. These issues are typically between parents who are not together. By caring for the child, you will find incidences that place you in challenging situations. There are other situations as well, such as those between grandparents and parents that can also place you in difficult situations. Here is one example of being caught in the middle:

❖ Lesson From the Field: Caught in the Middle

> At our graduation celebration one year, I had two divorced parents that chose graduation as the place and time to pass the child from mother to father for a month. Obviously with tensions already high, it became somewhat of a spectacle. Two other parents pointed it out to me wanting me to fix their issues. (Yes, the director is expected to fix everything including domestic disputes which happen on your watch.) I didn't address it because it didn't appear out of control at that time. After that the mother came up and wanted me to "chase" after the father and his current wife as they pulled out of the parking lot. She wanted to get back the graduation tassel that she wanted to keep for the child. I said I wasn't going to do that. She was clearly still emotional and now focused on me going after her ex-husband. I again said no and offered to get her another tassel. She didn't want a replacement. She said it wasn't the one he graduated in and she would never get it back.

Handling Phone Calls From Angry Parents

Parents who have concerns both small and large will call. At times these calls can be angry, aggressive, and heated. Start these phone calls by being a good listener. This can be very time consuming but it is important. Often parents are angry and just need to vent. Let them do it. Listen carefully and take notes to focus on the real issues. The angry calls may be filled with lots of conversation that isn't the heart of the issue. Once the parent has calmed down, it's time to focus on the real issues.

Although the list of potential complaints is endless, common complaints include:

- ✓ Issues with another child
- ✓ Issues with teachers
- ✓ A minor scratch or boo-boo which was discovered and wasn't reported to the parent
- ✓ Issues with policies
- ✓ Issues with discipline
- ✓ Anger at having to leave work to pick up ill children

Unless the situation is very clear and you already understand all the circumstances refrain from any apologies, admissions of guilt, or statements that you will fix it. Use this as an opportunity to obtain all of the parent's view. Let the parent know that you will "look into it" and then get back to her. Then you need to do just that. Talk to the staff involved to get a clear picture of what was happened. It is very common to find out that the parent has a less than accurate view of the situation.

After completing your own investigation, get back with the parent. Provide the results of your investigation. If there were mistakes on the center's part, let the parent know that you are correcting those things. If there were not mistakes on the center's part, then let her know that as well. Usually these things are worked out. Parents get over their anger and are able to move forward. There may be times when parents remain angry and even leave following an incident and your follow up conversation with them.

Knowing that you can't be there every minute, make sure that your staff members know how you would handle the situation. Have them specify and require parents to meet your rules and then back them up. I told my staff to: follow the policies and "blame me." In other words, they didn't have to defend the policies just enforce them. If parents questioned the policies, they were to say that it was "Dr. Busch's rules" and the parent should make a point to talk to me if they had any concerns over such rules. The job of staff members is difficult enough. Give them the information and support that they need to deal with difficult situations.

When parents do question your policies, make it clear through communications that you truly care about their children. Even when they disagree with you and even when they are angry, calmly explain why your policies and actions were done the way they were. Always include how it benefits their child and all of the children.

A good example is the case of enforcing health policies. Even though a parent may be unhappy that you will not allow their child to attend the center on a day that they are exhibiting symptoms of illness, they should understand when you explain how this policy is important so that fewer illnesses are spread through the center. Be sure to elaborate that this means when someone else is ill and isn't allowed to attend; their child is not exposed to illnesses. Parents often have a narrow view and are focused on their world and their child. It is important to explain your answers with respect to the benefits provided to them based on the centers policies. Details such as this can turn a negative situation into one with a more positive outcome.

There are many personalities of parents just as there are many personalities of children. Some are much easier to work with and there will be some that you just can't please no matter what you do. As always, establish clear policies; explain "why" these policies are in place; and stick to them. If a policy isn't working, change it but don't make exceptions to a policy that remains in place.

❖ Lesson From the Field: Some Parents Look for Issues

Melanie's father was often disagreeable which was in direct contrast to her very sweet mother. One Friday, he came to pick her up from our playground outside and took her to potty before going home. He them approached the teacher on duty and wanted to know why the toilet was not flushed. She explained that parents often have their children potty before going home and we couldn't control it if they chose not to require their child to flush the potty. Then he realized we had run out of toilet paper, another routine occurrence. The teacher went to get more toilet paper. He didn't like waiting and wanted to know why extra toilet paper wasn't kept in the bathroom. She explained that it usually was but we had run out in that location.

Next, he wanted to know why there was no soap or towels in the bathroom. She explained that we had the children wash their hands in the kitchen to prevent children playing in the soap and flushing the cloth towels down the toilet. He then stated "you just let them walk around everywhere with fecal material on their hands touching everything." She said "No sir, they go directly to the sink and wash their hands after going to the restroom. He wanted to know why we used cloth towels instead of paper. She explained that is more economical and environmentally friendly to not throw away all those paper towels. It seems some parents just want to be disagreeable.

There are even times where it is beneficial to "help parents choose another center." It is amazing how the majority of issues brought by parents are only brought by a small percentage. Unhappy parents who just can't be pleased within the structure of your center can bring a great deal of stress to the center. They make your staff uncomfortable; they cause constant problems; they are angry; and these are often the ones who are going to call in a complaint to the state regulatory agency.

You also will likely have parents who want to come in and tell you how to run the program. At these times, it is simply necessary to reinforce that you make the decisions and that you do what is best for all of the children. I've even had a parent accuse me of providing a better education to another child, in the same classroom, than her child received. The two children were in the same classroom, with the same teacher, and the same curriculum. Children may perform at different levels and with different results, but the program is the same for all children. Then there are those truly extreme cases that really seem like something from a bad made for television movie. The good news is these extreme cases are rare but on occasion you will come across situations parents create that are almost beyond belief.

❖ Lesson From the Field: The Great Schoenherr Incident

A parent who had a history of complaints became a real example of how bizarre things can become. As sometime happens, this parent waited for me to leave to unleash an anger episode on a staff member. At 6:05 PM, just after closing I received a call from the managing teacher. She was very upset that Ms. Schoenherr had yelled at her for approximately 15 minutes saying that her children had marks and scratches from our center that were not explained. Ms Schoenherr made statements like she was going to take pictures and she was going to have to take the children to the emergency room because of a skin irritation, possibly a rash the "size of a strawberry" on her oldest child. This was the beginning of her outburst and irate behaviors. She was very vocal about issues of scratches, bug bites, and rashes which she alleged all happened at the center.

Another parent witnessed the event and when he had spoken up to the fact that he didn't appreciate her inappropriate behavior in front of his daughter. She began yelling at him! I called Ms. Schoenherr that evening. She did not take her children to the emergency room. She waited on her ex-husband to make the determination. This is when she referred to the strawberry sized mark. She said that in addition to the first child's mark, there were marks on her other child's head.

Those marks, on the second child had been documented the day before when the younger child told two separate teachers that her older sibling had scratched her. (Remember those notes on how important it is to document marks, occurrences, and what children say. At that time, we needed those notes and had them.) The teacher on duty did verify that she had been required to stop these two siblings from physically fighting with each other the night before at closing time.

I evaluated the irrational behavior and documentation from another parent who witnessed the incident. I was very concerned about the safety and security of our school as our children's health and welfare were always my top priority. I determined it was necessary to call Ms. Schoenherr and inform her that she must not set foot on the grounds of my center again, and if she did, we would call the police department.

Ms. Schoenherr became very loud and confrontational on the phone when notified that she was not to be on center property again. She yelled at me and then put her ex-husband on the phone, who was also very irate. He yelled that his children were sick; we should be ashamed; and that I was taking it out on his ex-wife. At this point, I advised that I would also add his name to the list of those who are banned from the center out of concern for safety. I said I was going to hang up the phone and did. I didn't pick up the phone on their repeated efforts to call back and yell at me some more.

The following day was difficult and I never left the center. I kept a careful watch out and stayed from opening until closing time to ensure the safety of everyone there from these people with irrational behavior. I also wrote a check for all unused tuition for the children and that was mailed to the parent along with the children's belongings.

Did I know this one was going to be reported to the state and create an investigation? Absolutely! Was I prepared? Absolutely! I accurately documented all of the occurrences and asked each of the teachers, who were unfortunately in the middle of the situation, to do the same. The inspector showed up a few days later. I looked at her and said I knew why she was there and promptly handed over all of our documentation. She interviewed the teachers, reviewed the documentation, and we did not receive any violations from the incident … after all we hadn't made any regulatory mistakes.

Our life experiences always provide perspective. Gaining experience by learning more about the field through the work of others can become part of your own knowledge. My hope is that now that you've "experienced" this incident that when you have parent incidences you can compare them to this one and (hopefully) say "at least it wasn't as bad as that one."

When parents have continued issues, it is good to help direct them from the center. Such constant issues make it difficult on both the management and the staff. When parents get angry, they are more likely to choose to file a complaint even if it isn't legitimate. We knew this was the case in the previous example. We were trying to just coast along with this family until the end of the year when they were scheduled to leave the center. Obviously, waiting didn't work so well in this situation. There are times when the enrollment and tuition are absolutely not worth the stress of keeping some children and families enrolled.

Choose Friends Carefully

Keep a professional relationship with parents as much as possible. When working with parents on a regular basis it feels like you know them well. Friendships can evolve as you meet great people and work with their children on a regular basis. It can feel very much like having friends. Be very careful of actually establishing friendships with the parents of children. Things are wonderful as long as everything goes right with their child. It is amazing how quickly some of these same parents will turn against you when something happens that they don't like.

❖ Lesson from the Field: Friends Associated with the Center

In the early years, as I established my childcare business, I was not as hardened to the realities of the business. I was shocked a few times when parents who I considered friends made complete 180 degree turns, as soon as something happened that they didn't like. I began very open and took things personally. I quickly learned to harden up my defenses and take very little personally.

I do have some wonderful friends that I met through my childcare business that I remain in touch with today. There aren't a lot of them. I enjoyed the company of many but counted very few as friends due to the often harsh realities of the business. You will develop friendships over time but proceed cautiously.

Making Tough Choices

There are times when you inevitably are put into a bad situation by parents. These can fall under a number of contexts. A common concern centers on divorced parents who do not get along well. When there are custody issues, it is very important to require a copy of custody papers to be on file. The center can't keep a custodial parent from taking the child from the center. This is important. Just because the mother states that the father isn't allowed to take the child doesn't mean that you can enforce that. Require legal papers to determine any parental rights issues.

There are numerous situations which put the center's management and staff in uncomfortable situations. These often stem from family issues and by nature of caring for the children, the center's employees become mixed in the middle of situations they do not want to be in.

❖ Lesson from the Real World: Sheldon's Father

> *Sheldon's parents were going through a divorce and related custody issues. His mother was often afraid that his father would come and pick him up from school. The father would call and ask if he was there almost daily. On one occasion during the middle of the custody issues, the father did arrive to pick him up. We weren't comfortable with the situation. What did we do? We had to let him go with the father. He had legal rights as a parent as both parents still had custody. We did the only thing that we could do under the circumstances which was call the mother and let her know that the father had picked up the child.*

Another difficult topic is that of investigating abuse issues with parents. Be aware of legal requirements with regard to the care and safety of children. If staff members at the center suspect a child is being abused or neglected, they have an obligation to report such suspicion to the appropriate authorities for investigation. The childcare center staff is an advocate for the health, safety, and security of all of the children in care. Reporting child abuse or neglect concerns is not an option; it is an absolute legal and ethical responsibility.

18

Financial Management

In this chapter, you will investigate the important details which contribute to successful financial management in the childcare setting including:

- Overview of Financial Management
- Profitability and Size
- Overhead and Labor Costs
- Business Cycles
- Controlled Growth
- What Really Counts
- Financial Strategies for Small Centers

Overview of Financial Management

Financial management is of great importance. It is absolutely necessary to organize your financial management strategies; spend time completing important tasks; and review your business spreadsheets. Look at the expenses both in terms of dollar amounts and in terms of percentage rates. If you don't review your budgets and pay attention to your finances, it is quite likely that these will not be very good. In addition, if you don't accurately track your revenues and expenses, how will you know if your business is profitable much less if you are maximizing your profit margin? Yes, this chapter is where we leave the concepts of heart, children, and curriculum to fully evaluate the business end of childcare. After all it doesn't matter how great your program is, if you can't make money doing it, it's not a viable business and your center will not stay open.

Profitability and Size

Childcare is known for low profit margins and a need to be big to have good profitability. Although it may be easier to make more money with a larger center and larger enrollment, the reality is that small centers can be profitable as well. I always took seriously the financial end of the program and managed to take a relatively small and specialized center into a profit margin that far exceeded many larger centers.

With this in mind, create a quality program that has real value to offer families and price your program accordingly. Aiming to be the "cheapest in town" will help fill up your roster, but it will not necessarily provide you with a profitable and sustainable business. Strive to create a quality program that is affordable for your target market and provides your children with an exceptional early childhood education.

❖ Lesson From the Field: Competing on Price

At a conference a few years ago, some of owners got into a discussion about continuing to cut their tuition rates. They found it necessary to cut tuition rates because the other centers around them were continuing to reduce rates, due to economic conditions. This was obviously leading to financial problems for the centers. It is a perfect example of why programs should not be competing to be the cheapest in the area. Without tuition rates which support the business, owners are not able to attract and retain staff, purchase appropriate materials, and some may even find they are unable to pay the bills. This is an example of a downward spiral that can potentially lead to closing the business.

The same holds true of larger centers. Even with all of the additional tuition coming into the center. If finances are not carefully measured and evaluated, you will likely have a poor return on your investment and certainly not meet your income earning potential. By nature, the childcare industry is a service industry and it is labor cost intensive. Every time you add more children and more tuition, you also add significant expenses as you must have the space, the materials, recordkeeping requirements, and the qualified staff to support your growth.

Overhead and Labor Costs

In the early stages of development, whether you are starting a center from scratch or purchasing an existing center, careful consideration should be placed on the cost of overhead. Pay close attention to the cost of the building. Having a grand scale and beautiful center is really tempting. It looks impressive; parents will love the appearance; and you will most likely be able to charge a higher tuition than smaller less visually impressive centers. However, be aware of how many more children you will need to enroll as well as how much more you will need to charge in order to meet those costs.

Capacity is another area. Having a large center which is licensed for and supports a high capacity gives the "potential" for greater income. Potential is the key word. Look at the market carefully. Think about how long it will take to reach that capacity. Will you be able to fill all of those empty spots in your center? If you are not able to fill those spots, you will still be paying for the grand space that you are providing to a smaller number of children.

Business Cycles

Most industries have relatively predictable business cycles. Be aware of the business cycle for your center. This particular cycle can vary from center to center based on your particular market, location, and other determining factors.

The typical business cycle for childcare revolves around the school year. In the summer you are likely to see a lower enrollment as some children graduate from preschool programs and move into other programs. This can be fairly typical even if you offer school-age programs. At this point in time, some parents will find alternative and often cheaper forms of childcare including teenage babysitters, camp type programs, grandparents, or other options that are more readily available in summer. Also, parents who are not working (if you provide part-time programs) will often take their children out of educational and part-time programs to keep them home for the summer. This can impact your total enrollment at the beginning of summer. Summer is also a time new children will likely fill some of those spots as their parents also see summer as a logical time to make changes.

August brings another change as your school age children go back into their public or private school programs and are with you only before and after school rather than for the entire day. This decreases the tuition rate for those children from a full day to a part-time program. You will often see this beginning of your new school year as a prime time to advertise and bring new children into your program for the next school year. During the fall, programs tend to continue to build. Not all parents of younger children are ready to start in August. Some will just begin to think of their child's education for the next year at that time and then will begin the process of looking for a new place. Use all of the methods discussed in Chapter 22: Sustaining Long Term Success, to build your enrollment at this time. After you have built your program, the school year will often continue on a fairly predictable enrollment with only small numbers of children enrolling or withdrawing until summer time.

Another factor in financial management is determining tuition payments. Tuition is typically paid each week. Keep in mind that there is a great deal of bookkeeping associated with depositing; crediting to accounts; checking on late payments; contacting parents; and collecting late payments and other related fees. If it is feasible for the parents in your center, consider adjusting tuition to a bi-monthly or even monthly charge. Some centers will even include discounts for paying the full month in advance. Requiring fewer payments is a cost saver in terms of reducing the number of times you have to do all of those tasks associated with collecting tuition.

Another concept to consider is how often you pay your employees. It works under the same principle. If employees are paid every two weeks instead of every week, you have reduced the amount of time it takes totaling hours, determining over-time, and printing paychecks. If you are having payroll outsourced, it won't save you time. It should however, save money by reducing how many times the process has to be completed. Keep in mind that if you are paying your staff every other week, twice per calendar year you will make payroll three times in one month. Be prepared and have that money set aside and ready. If you choose to pay bi-monthly, your payments will be more even but over-time calculations will be more cumbersome, as they may be determined by the hours split between two different paychecks.

Taxes are due on particular schedules. There are numerous taxes that a small business is responsible for. This is where it is best to hire a good small business CPA to have all of your records set up correctly and be aware of all of your necessary tax filings. Once this is done, determine when those expenses are scheduled to occur. Put these on your calendar and prepare your budget for those times as well. An easy way to do this is to determine how much money needs to be set aside each month to be put toward these expenses.

Controlled Growth

When things are going well, you are enrolling children to your licensed capacity, and building a waiting list because even more families want to join you. Proceed with caution! Growth can be a wonderful thing. It can lead to greater profits and a stronger business; however, growing too fast can lead to just the opposite. Keep in mind that in order to grow a childcare business, you generally must add space. Construction and expansion can be very expensive. Can you fund the expansion with your own capital or will you need a bank loan to do this? How much additional debt are you willing to take on? Will you be able to continue to manage the payments in the event that enrollment drops unexpectedly? An example of a sudden and unexpected drop would be if a brand new center opens in your town serving the same target market that you do. Another example would be a severe economic downturn.

In addition to expanding your center and likely your debt, you will need to hire more staff to care for the new children. All of these costs can be justified provided you are able to fill those rooms. If those rooms are not filled with enough children to pay for the additional costs, your income will actually decrease. This is often the case when expanding as it will take time to build the enrollment for these additional places that you have created. I always stated that when expanding, I "went backwards for awhile" before moving forward again.

That is not to say that expanding isn't good. It can be an excellent choice if it is carefully evaluated; finances support the additional costs; the market is right; and you are ready to take on the extra load. As always in childcare, expansion is complex and adding more children means making sure you can hire more quality staff, handle more children, more paperwork, and more parents without decreasing quality. Centers which expand too quickly, often wind up sacrificing the quality of their programs to keep up with the realities of the increased enrollment.

What Really Counts

Whatever size is right for you, build your program on quality, great teachers, and the highest level of care. These are what really make a great center. It's not the huge space or brand new facilities. If you can afford to and choose to create a large center with beautiful spaces, it can work. These elements are nice and will attract attention. Put your pen to paper and determine what you can comfortably afford without over extending. Don't commit to overhead that you may not be able to manage.

Lower overhead and smaller facilities create the opportunity to offer your service in smaller towns which may have fewer established licensed centers. This method also allows specialization. Owners that choose to operate smaller centers can create a market niche which is not already being met in the area. This type of center can offer specialized programs and charge higher rates for excellent programs. Small childcare centers can be very profitable based on specialization and lower overhead.

❖ Lesson From the Field: Slow Growth and Attention to Quality

I owned and operated a small childcare center. I started out with minimal debt and on a small operations scale. I was able to get the business into the black after only one year even with a small enrollment and specialty programs. We then proceeded to expand our space to allow for additional children. It was still small by most standards, but it was based on careful choices which centered on low building costs. These choices led to a good business model which produced a profit margin well above the industry average. I utilized a philosophy of exceptional programs that provided a great benefit to children, lean operational costs, and a no waste management style. It provided a good example of how designing and operating for a niche market can be a good business strategy.

Make sure that a great deal of thought and sufficient resources are put toward the children's furnishings and materials. It is relatively common to see a brand new beautiful building that has minimal children's toys, activities, and furnishings. Don't run out of finances before putting in the things that the children need for a good daily experience. Include lots of toys, activities, art materials, and other things for children to have happy active days filled with learning.

As a part of financial management, it is appropriate to set a supply fee to be paid by parents either annually or for each term. This fee should then be used solely for the benefit of supplies for the children. These supplies can be in the form of both consumable supplies (art materials, paper, and workbooks); shelf materials (learning activities and toys); and even for playground equipment. Just make sure, if you charge a fee, that the parents and children get the benefit. Don't charge a fee for the basic day to day operations of the business. Tuition rates should cover these things.

❖ Lesson From the Field: Supply Fees

Enrollment in my center included a supply fee for the school year (August-May) and a separate one for the summer. These fees were used to purchase consumable materials that the children used. The fees were used for educational materials and projects throughout the year. Children went home almost every day with "work" in their hands from lesson materials, art projects, and cooking projects. The children were proud of their work and the parents could see all of the good things they were doing on a daily basis.

I chose to apply an upfront supply fee rather than "nickel and dime" parents and collect small amounts of money for each project. It worked better. Parents saw all the great supplies their children used, the learning activities, and fun art projects that all went home. In addition, we included two family events per year. The final event was a picnic and graduation in May where all parents, friends, and family were invited at no additional charge.

As a part of good financial management, review your tuition rates and if appropriate raise them slightly each year. The cost of operating a center almost always increases every year. Raising rates by a very small amount, even 1%-2% per year, will allow the rates to gradually increase overtime and keep up with increasing costs. This method also sets the center up so that you never have to have big increases in tuition rates. Remember, simply by providing annual raises for your great staff members that you need to retain, your operational costs will increase. In addition, almost everything else goes up some each year including food, materials, and bills.

These tuition increases are most valuable when your center is at or near capacity. In a low enrollment year, keep in mind that you can increase your center's revenue more effectively by focusing on increasing the enrollment and filling those empty chairs in your center. When enrollment is low, it is best to not raise tuition.

Payroll is one of the largest costs in childcare centers whether it is a large center or a small center. While analyzing payroll costs, remember the greatest contributor of all to a quality early childhood education program is the staff. This includes both the administrators and the teachers that you put into the classroom with the children. Hire carefully, train staff, and promote those who really contribute to your program. Include regular performance reviews and pay increases. These teachers are the "face" of your center. They are the ones that make your day to day operations successful and provide great programs. Pay the best wages that you are able to pay. This is a financial investment in the heart of your business.

Financial Strategies for Small Centers

The concepts of specialization of your center and charging higher tuition rates than other more traditional childcare centers in the area were previously discussed. In addition, there are a number of strategies to increase profitability in smaller centers. Cost cutting strategies in smaller centers include doing work which is often outsourced in larger centers.

Can you or your staff members:

- ✓ Do your own bookkeeping
- ✓ Fix your own stopped up toilets
- ✓ Paint walls and shelves
- ✓ Mow the grass
- ✓ Grocery shop
- ✓ Clean the building
- ✓ Shampoo carpets

Many of these things are hired out to other companies and have the impact of adding large amounts to the expenses on your income statement. Choose the things that are feasible to do in house and either do them or assign them to staff members. These will keep your costs lower and relate to an increase in that all important "bottom line" on the income statement.

❖ Lesson From the Field: Simple Steps to Reducing Expenses

For the most part teachers in my center cleaned their own rooms and those who closed did the final room cleanings that were left. In addition, we made simple changes over time such as using "wash cloths" instead of paper towels for drying hands. We bought cheap wash cloths in volume packages at the local discount store. They worked better for drying hands than the paper towels. We would simply wash and bleach several loads of these hand towels each day. As they became frayed and old, we purchased more and put the ragged ones in a different pile for one use applications such as cleaning up blood from a scraped knee or cleaning up a very messy diaper that needed more than a diaper wipe. Then the soiled towels went into the trash can.

It was easy and made a huge difference. This one step cut out the purchasing, transporting, and storing of volumes of boxes of paper towels. This cut costs significantly and it literally cut the trash we produced in half! It was better financially and much better environmentally. Not only did we use this strategy to save costs and reduce trash, we then let parents and potential parents know about our "environmentally friendly" strategies. This strategy did require the purchase of a washer and dryer but these are things that most centers will need to invest in once they are able to do so. The equipment paid for itself over time with the cost savings.

Tuition management should be put on a regular schedule. This requires documenting paid tuition and checking for late tuition on a regular (often weekly) basis. Make sure that this is done diligently. Have a written policy of when tuition is due, late fees, and how long you will continue to provide services before the child is dismissed from your program. This can be the "ugly" side of childcare at times, but it is a business. If you don't require payment and enforce a deadline, some people won't pay.

Being able to do your own bookkeeping and payroll can also be good money saving strategies. One of the best parts is the financial data is always at your finger tips. You know where you are both in expenses and income. This isn't the best strategy for everyone but for those who like to see the numbers and keep their hands on the finances, it is a really good area to do yourself. With the purchase of standard business software and payroll programs it is not difficult to take care of the bookkeeping in house. Business taxes are a different concept all together. It is best to hire a certified public accountant for all business tax planning and filing.

Will you allow one or a few of your staff members to have a business credit card? If yes, make sure that they have to sign a credit card statement that they are responsible for all charges made on the credit card. They must produce receipts for each time the credit card is used, and it is only to be used for authorized business purchases. Saying all that, it is still possible that even someone you trust will make unauthorized charges to the credit card. It is disappointing to find that cards have been used for personal use by someone you trusted.

Employees, even though they signed to be responsible for the purchases on the card, may not have enough money to cover their personal charges on the card. Whether by mistake or intentional, the misuse of a business card by an employee creates problems for the business. If you choose to allow employees credit cards, keep this in mind. Place appropriate limits on the employees' cards to reduce the dollar amount that can be charged to that card. One additional benefit of doing your own books is that you are likely to find any financial concerns more quickly than if someone else is doing them for you. This includes increases in costs, incorrect charges to your account, and even personal charges placed by employees on their business cards.

If you choose not to provide a credit card and not to be at the center every minute that it is open, there is another option. Gift cards could do the trick for most relevant expenses. These could be in the form of general cards such as bank cards like Visa or MasterCard Gift Cards. The employee must still provide the receipt to show what the purchase was for and to provide the documentation for your records. The real benefit is that you can determine exactly how much is on the cards and use multiple cards so that the total value on any one card provided to an employee is lower. Grocery store cards are another great option. It seems like much of the purchasing that needs to be done revolves around either food or project supplies. A gift card to a local discount store such as Wal-Mart where purchases can be made for food, center needs, and craft supplies would be a good choice.

For times when you will not be available, such as a vacation, consider what to do if something had to be done immediately such as a heater going out in the building. If you have an employee that you can trust with a credit card, this is one option. Another option is to have a temporary signature card on file with your bank for your CPA, or bookkeeping professional, to write a check on your behalf in such an emergency.

Whether you choose to do your own bookkeeping or to outsource this job, make sure your books are accurate. Only claim true expenses of the business. Some small business owners will become lenient with their "business expenses" and charge home and personal expenses to the business. Keep the books clean and accurate. Hire a CPA who knows you and your business and can offer financial advice that is valuable for the ongoing success of your business. Use these strategies and then you don't have to worry about audits of your business books. As with all other aspects of your business, complete your financial records with the highest degree of quality and care.

19

Records Management

In this chapter, you will look into the vast and often complex world of records management in childcare including:

- Records Management Overview
- The Office
- Calendars and Checklists
- Student Records
- Confidential Records

Records Management Overview

As you review state records of violations for childcare facilities, make a note of how frequently citations involve recordkeeping. The recordkeeping required by regulations can be huge. There are many areas of recordkeeping along with requirements to update them frequently. Based on this, many centers do not adequately keep up with the required demands of recordkeeping. It can cost them many citations in a single inspection! Records are a part of almost every inspection. You can expect your inspector to request specific records along with a sampling of personnel and student records to make sure that you are in compliance at each inspection. Recordkeeping for the purpose of state audits during an investigation is detailed in Chapter 3: State Childcare Regulations and Records. In this chapter we will focus primarily on the recordkeeping for the purpose of business operations and office management issues.

The Office

Remember much of the financial data that passes across your desk should be kept confidential. Don't leave papers and records lying around which shouldn't be accessible to everyone. Have a locked file to store all financial data in. Even when you trust your employees, do not get lax in confidentiality issues. The sad part is that some will disappoint you and there will be some who feel free to "snoop."

Why not just lock the office door? Childcare brings on a very different type of recordkeeping issue. Volumes of files and records must be accessible to the state inspector at all times. These files also contain emergency care information for the children in care that may need to be accessed by the staff on duty. Yet these same files must be kept confidential. What does that mean? It means that you have to keep the files in a secured area, usually the office, and limit access to those files. At the same time such rules also mean that you can't lock these files in an office and go away from the center. These include the staff and children's records that must be accessible.

Now we just created a situation which means that unless the director is there every minute of every hour that the center is open, others must be allowed in the office. Typically those allowed in the office should be named and be the ones who are left in charge during the director's absence. Even so, you must leave the office unlocked or the files out and accessible. Based on this, it is important that the director have a locked closet or file cabinet in order to keep all confidential financial records locked up at all times. Your financial records, payroll records, etc., are generally not something that is auditable by the state childcare licensing agency.

Calendars and Checklists

Childcare is a highly regulated industry with high liability concerns. This means that along with all of the other typical business forms and filings, there is also a large volume of additional paperwork to manage. Creating checklists and schedules is essential to maintaining all of the required paperwork. Create a checklist which includes time frames based on the routine requirements for your business needs and for your state regulatory paperwork.

Examples of state licensing records which require managing and scheduled updating include:

- ✓ Enrollment paperwork and re-enrollment if it is required annually
- ✓ Allergies and special needs and annual updates on these
- ✓ Parents contact information and scheduled updates to ensure accuracy
- ✓ Menus
- ✓ Vaccination requirements
- ✓ Hearing and vision screenings
- ✓ Health updates
- ✓ Staff background checks and renewals
- ✓ Staff professional development
- ✓ Drivers license renewals for drivers
- ✓ Insurance renewals
- ✓ Annual fire inspections
- ✓ Sanitation inspections

- ✓ Gas pipe inspections
- ✓ City permit renewals

Some of these requirements fall under both a local regulations and state childcare regulations. Many state regulations require compliance with local regulations. In such cases, documentation of all local requirements must be provided to your state childcare licensing. In addition, there are records which you need maintained that may not be required by the state. These records need to be updated and documented regularly for the benefit of your business operations.

Examples of business records and documentation updates include:

- ✓ Bill payment schedules
- ✓ Staff schedules
- ✓ Payroll schedules
- ✓ Curriculum schedules
- ✓ Curriculum preparation
- ✓ Purchases of materials for lessons, activities, and special projects
- ✓ Parties and planning for such activities
- ✓ Food purchasing
- ✓ Children's birthdays
- ✓ Vehicle maintenance
- ✓ Interior cleaning schedules
- ✓ Building maintenance schedules
- ✓ Performance reviews and raise evaluations
- ✓ Staff disciplinary reviews
- ✓ Tuition due dates
- ✓ Checks for late tuition or unpaid tuition
- ✓ Parent communication
- ✓ Newsletters
- ✓ Tax filings for local, state, and federal taxes

Both types of records will need scheduling time frames. Some of these will be done weekly. Others will be done monthly, semi-monthly, quarterly, and annually. Create a schedule which is feasible and make checklists based on that schedule to keep all of the paperwork processed and managed appropriately. This is a very important part of managing a successful center. Keeping the paperwork on schedule and completed on time will mean that all of your federal requirements are met, your state and childcare regulations are met, and you are in good standing with the local government requirements as well.

The final note regarding keeping on top of records through scheduling is to be aware that over time state childcare regulations and local code requirements may change. Make sure to include such changes in your designed schedule. The scheduling and paperwork portion of the job, just like the other parts, is not stable. It must be updated to accommodate changes and additional criteria that you are required to meet.

Student Records

Individual student records must be maintained on every child enrolled in the center. State agencies usually provide enrollment forms which will have all of the regulatory requirements included if these are completely filled out. Not only must these forms be complete at enrollment, these files must be updated at least once a year. The information such as parents' contact numbers, addresses, and other details may change over time. For children who stay with your center for years, this can change numerous times. In addition, this is your opportunity to look at any changes in the child's health such as added restrictions or new allergies that came to light after the child was enrolled. A good time to calendar the updates is when children are signing up for the next school year.

Daily attendance records must be accurately recorded and maintained by the center. Create a system for signing children in and out and make sure it is done for every child every day. This system can be as elaborate as a purchased computer program that parents utilize or as simple as a roll sheet that is maintained by the teacher in the classroom. Keep these records for months or even years. Refer to your own state regulations for specific requirements for maintaining such records at your center.

Student accident and illness reports should be completed and carefully documented for every occurrence. These simple reports should be written for every minor boo-boo that occurs on your premises. Children are busy and active. Different parents have greatly varied reactions. Accidents will happen. Some parents will not be upset even for bigger accidents. These parents are understanding and do not blame the center when the child has an accident. Other parents will react strongly even for the most minor scratches or other boo-boos. Document all accidents as if the parents overreact.

Call the parents immediately for any significant accidents. Call the parents who over react, even for those little minor incidences. Document phone calls to parents on the accident form and have the parent sign the form when they arrive at the center. This is your proof that the parent was told of the incident. If you get to the end of the day and realize that someone didn't have the accident report signed and the child has already been signed out for the day, call the parent. Let her know, even if it was just a little scratch. Then document the phone call on the form and have the form signed by the parent the next day. It may sound obsessive, but this level of attention to parent communication and documentation is very important on those few times when a parent becomes very angry and chooses to call the state and initiate an investigation ... or worse files a lawsuit against the center.

Student accident reports are often required, by the state regulations, to remain in the child's folder for a specified amount of time. After this time, these can be moved into an archived or locked records area. These should be maintained so that there is documentation should an issue arise later regarding an incident or injury which happened at the center.

Keep daily notes in a spiral notebook or other form where teachers can date and note specific events. This documentation is valuable from a liability standpoint. If a child says something happened and shows something as simple as a bruise when he arrives at school. Make a note.

There may be instances where parents make accusations that something happened at school when it happened outside of school. The documentation will be valuable in supporting that the bruises or injuries happened outside of the center. These types of accusations can happen under different circumstances but are more likely when a child's parents are not living together. For example, if something happened during one parent's care, the other parent may not know this until picking the child up after school on her day of custody. Document, document, document … it never hurts to write down the facts and it may be very valuable at some point in time.

❖ Lesson From the Field: Documenting Children's Issues

I had a wonderful first aid and CPR instructor who would come to the center and provide all of our safety related training. She described the importance of documenting injuries with this example: If a child says that she hurt her arm over the weekend and is complaining about it, make a note of this including the date and time. Her example was that the child had cracked the bone prior to coming to school and then put pressure on it while at school and finished breaking the arm. The parent then says the arm was broken at school. It is important to have that documentation that there was an injury prior to walking through your doors.

Confidential Records

There is a big distinction between state licensed childcare records and business records. As discussed, there are specific records required in the childcare center. These records must be accessible to the staff member who is in charge at the time so that they have all of the emergency information for the children. It must also be accessible to an unannounced state licensing inspector or state licensing investigator who may show up at any time during the facilities licensed operating hours.

Confidential childcare records are different. These records include discipline notes to parents; behavioral concerns and incidences; documentation kept on children for your own liability protection; notes from parents; tuition information from parents; and other records that you want or need to keep. Generally these are not required by childcare licensing. (As always, regulations vary by state, check your own state regulations regarding required records.) As a general rule, if it is not required by your state licensing agency and it's not standard information kept on every child, then it doesn't need to be in the accessible file.

As a general rule, the state regulations have to do with the safety and care of children and some very basic requirements for the business entity such as the requirement for insurance and meeting local codes. Over and above these items is your "business" which is regulated by business law but is not part of the regulations of childcare licensing. Business and finance records should be kept confidential and stored in the locked area. Business expenses, receipts, bills, payroll, profit and loss statements, and other such records are for the benefit of the owners. Keep accurate business records and store them in a locked area. These do not need to be accessible to staff members, parents, or state licensing representatives.

Keep in mind the importance of payroll confidentiality as well. Do not store your payroll information in your standard staff file which is accessible. Rates of pay are between the owner and employee. This brings up another consideration. Some employees will be needing employment validation for things such as renting an apartment, purchasing a vehicle, or even when looking for a new job. You will get phone requests for such confidential information. Don't give out any employee data without making sure this is what the employee wants. It is best to get that permission in writing.

You will also have access to confidential information through background checks required for employment. Texas background checks include both a standard state background check along with fingerprinting. Once the background checks have cleared, keep the records in your files. This provides a back-up system in case the state doesn't have the verification. Mistakes do happen with regard to agencies and paperwork. Keep your copies!

❖ Lesson From the Field: Conflicting Regulations

There are times when regulations even within a particular agency conflict. One such area that I experienced was that of background checks. On occasion a background check came back with an arrest on it but it wasn't an arrest which would disqualify an individual from working in childcare. In such cases, it was at the center's discretion whether to continue with the hire or not. I saw numerous things that I wouldn't accept; however, the one that was most frequent was the prosecution for a bad check. I had wonderful employees who had at one time accidently written a check that bounced ... at times this occurrence was showing from many years ago. The real issue is that the information was confidential. The notice from the state said that if you shared that information, you could be held liable for that breach of confidentiality.

Where did I keep it? I kept it in a special file hidden deep back inside a desk drawer packed full of non-confidential files. Only two other people knew where that file was and what was in it. They were not even allowed to look at it and didn't know who the information related to. It was never to be accessed unless we were required to show it under a state inspection or investigations.

One final note on financial concerns is the necessity of a shredder. Purchase a shredder and shred all documents which contain confidential information. This includes not only financial data, but also information on job applicants, children, and staff. Keep the shredder in a safe location away from the children's areas. Keep it turned off and unplugged or stored away when not in use. As with every aspect of this business, the children's safety should always be on your mind. Children can be severely injured by a shredder. Never allow children access to the shredder.

20

Facilities Management

In this chapter, you will investigate the realities of effective facilities management including:

- Facilities Management Overview
- Maintaining a Quality Center
- Quality Furniture
- Equipment
- Children's Materials
- Facility Updates While Operational
- Maintaining the Outdoor Space
- Handling Emergencies and Disruptions
- Temporary Closures

Facilities Management Overview

One of the most exciting things when establishing a center is to see the beautiful environment. All the fresh paint, new flooring, shelves filled with perfect educational materials and new toys create a wonderful and inviting environment. It's one of the reasons that a brand new center (or newly renovated) is so impressive. It looks beautiful and makes a positive impression on parents and children. The challenge comes later as you work to continue this wonderful environment after you have children in care every day.

If you have children at home, you know that they can be a little difficult on your house … bringing in dirt on their shoes; spills on the carpet; potty training messes; and illnesses resulting in vomit on the floor. Now picture your home with 40 children, or 100 children, or over 200. In addition, you have at least one parent coming in and out with each child daily. Having this many people in one building definitely requires major attention in the area of maintaining the center.

Maintaining a Quality Center

Maintaining a quality environment is a much bigger challenge than establishing one. A successful center includes many children, staff members, and even family members joining you in the building during the day. This constant use can really damage a center if consistent maintenance and good supervision of the children is not maintained.

Perhaps the single most important step in maintaining a nice environment is good supervision by the teachers in the classrooms. Careful supervision is needed to insure that the children are doing appropriate activities and are not damaging the center. A structured or semi-structured indoor center environment also lends itself to less damage by children. In structured environments children have more strict rules on what they are doing and are used to following rules. In a less hectic environment and one with lower student to teacher ratios it is easier for teachers to stop children before they damage materials and facilities.

❖ Lesson From the Field: Damages and Supervision

My center was a structured children's environment; however, even in a structured environment, children can quickly damage property if not carefully supervised. During play time one day, several children peeled a large area of paint off the wall while the teacher was clearly not supervising carefully.

Even in centers with good supervision and well behaved children, toys and materials will be damaged along with walls, floors, and furniture. The volume of use takes a toll on the building and the materials. Some cleaning has to be done throughout the entire day. Floors need to be swept or vacuumed, bathrooms need to be cleaned, and eating surfaces need to be sanitized. Regular maintenance extends beyond basic cleaning and includes keeping the center looking nice and in good repair.

Smells or offensive odors are one of the biggest complaints that people have when walking into a center. Smell alone can convince someone coming to learn about your program that the center isn't clean. Pay attention to cleanliness in both appearance and in smell. Restrooms should be cleaned multiple times a day (not left for a cleaning crew that comes in each night). This includes regularly scheduled cleanings along with extra cleanings for all those times when children "miss" the toilet.

Trash with stinky diapers should go out often. If it stinks up the entire room (and some diapers will), it should be taken out immediately. Never allow bad smells to permeate your rooms. No one wants to work in a dirty or smelly environment. Also, be aware that the person inside the room may not be fully aware of the odors. This is the job for the director as she makes her rounds to be sure the rooms look and smell good. Basic cleaning goes on all day every day.

❖ Lesson From the Field: The Value of Good Cleaning Equipment

One of the best investments I made was the purchase of a commercial grade carpet cleaner. I wasn't able to do this until I had been open several years. During the first few years, I

rented one periodically. By owning one and having it available all the time, my staff and I were able to keep the entire center much cleaner. In addition to cleaning carpets on a regular schedule, we were able to pull it out and deep clean every time a child vomited on the carpet and every time a child couldn't make it to the restroom fast enough and had a potty training "oops!"

Quality Furniture

Whenever possible try to purchase commercial grade or high quality furniture. These will usually last longer and give you more value for your dollar over time. These products are however, more expensive. When the center is just getting started it may be necessary to purchase less expensive furnishings and just be aware that these items may need replacing sooner.

Children's furniture is an area in which owners and directors should take great care in choosing. Good furniture for small children should include making sure that there aren't sharp edges which can cut or injure a child if they fall into the furniture. Ensure that the furniture is stable and doesn't pose a tipping hazard. A shelf filled with materials which is not stable can severely injure a small child. Keep in mind it is a group environment which creates additional potential hazards, as children may push or lean on furnishings and knock them into or on another child.

With this in mind take the details of furniture one step further; make sure each piece is well placed within the center so that it is less likely to become a hazard. An example is a bookshelf which is placed against a wall is less likely to be pushed over than one placed in the center of the room where children can get behind it. Think through all of your furniture, materials, and overall center layout to create the safest environment possible.

Equipment

Your budget should include money for the replacement of equipment as needed. Set some money aside because equipment does go out and it can be very inconvenient. Just as with other products, typical household appliances and equipment will not have the same life expectancy in a childcare center as they will in a home environment. The options are to purchase regular appliances such as dishwashers, washers, and dryers and understand that they have a shorter life expectancy or purchase commercial equipment at a much greater initial capital outlay. The right choice on such items depends on both the financial situation of the center when these have to be purchased, along with the number of children enrolled which correlates to how much usage the appliance will get. Facilities with small numbers of children will be able to manage with household appliances. If you choose to purchase household appliances, rather than commercial, be aware that most manufacturers' warrantees are voided when it is used in a commercial facility.

Equipment and fixtures get very heavy use in a childcare center. Toilets fall under this area. It is a fairly regular occurrence for toilets to overflow. Children regularly overfill toilets with loads of paper ... even entire rolls including the cardboard base. This instigates the necessity of not only unstopping the toilet but grabbing those plastic gloves and taking much of that paper back out of the toilet. It's not all going down. Is there a good time for toilet overflows? No, but there are certainly times that are worse than others such as during the middle of parties with all of the parents and grandparents. In a center with many children … expect the unexpected.

- ❖ Lesson From the Field: Plumbing Problems

    At one point, we had major plumbing problems. The pipes stopped up and the toilets overflowed much more than usual. We had looked at various possible causes and tried to address those repairs; however, the problem continued. I called a plumber to evaluate the problem. At first he didn't see anything as it worked while he was there. I insisted he look further that there was a problem somewhere. He wound up going into the pipes from the outdoors and then told me to come and look! He had never seen anything like this in all of his years as a plumber!

    I went outside where the pipes were opened and saw that he had pulled many of our cloth hand towels out of the pipes. A child had been flushing cloth towels down the toilet. Lots of them! We did locate the child who had done this. In response, we moved the towels and hand washing outside of the actual restroom and into a supervised area to prevent further problems.

Why do the toilets overflow often? One of the main challenges to regulating toilet problems is that this is the one room in the building where children are allowed to have privacy. That means that they not only make judgment mistakes, but sometimes have a little too much fun in there!

Children's Materials

As for children's materials, have your teachers not only supervise the behavior of children but teach them how to take care of their toys and educational materials. This is an important lesson in early childhood. It needs to be directly taught to children. Even when children are taught to be careful with materials and generally take care of their materials, these items have a somewhat limited life. Materials which are built for commercial use will most often last longer.

Even with good care, these materials won't last forever. Include in your budget to replace a certain amount of the children's materials each year. Consistency is the key to maintaining toys and materials for children. Buy some new ones every year and remove those that are damaged, stained, or otherwise not in good condition. Purchasing some new each year, keeps good materials on the shelves for children. They absolutely need these materials for a good early childhood program. Books are included in this category. There are directors who decide not to replace materials, particularly books, because they "just get torn up." Buy age appropriate books including cloth books for babies, cardboard books for toddlers, and standard books for children three and older. Some items will be torn up but in the process many children will also be learning how to take care of the books.

Facility Updates While Operational

There are some maintenance processes and center updates which are difficult to complete while operational. Replacement of flooring, painting the walls, electrical updates, and other things which would interfere with daily operations prove challenging. Power being shut off, paint fumes and mess, and workers in the building are all challenges that are faced when making major renovations; and yet these types of updates must be done periodically if the center is going to maintain its quality and nice appearance. Some of these such as replacing heating and cooling systems are beyond aesthetics and are required to operate in compliance with licensing standards.

These often have to be done on the weekends or evenings and it can be difficult to find people to do the work on those time frames. In addition, it may be costly when requiring workers to be there during hours that the center is closed. Take care choosing when you will proceed and how you will implement these things when needed. It can take longer and be more costly when trying to work around your hours of operation.

- ❖ Lesson From the Field: New Carpet

    We had new carpet installed over a weekend. New additions, including carpet, can produce a strong odor inside the center. Our parents were thrilled with the updates and we didn't have any problems; however, there are incidences at other centers of parents reporting such things to the state as a complaint.

- ❖ Lesson From the Field: Painting Updates

    Our center needed painting updates after about six years into business. I hired painters that would work almost all night each night. It was challenging as we moved furniture each night for painters and replaced everything each day for our activities. In addition, there was the odor of new paint. Again, our parents were very patient and loved the updates and the clean look of new paint colors on the walls.

Most parents are happy that the center is being updated and appreciate the attention put toward maintaining a quality center. There will always be someone who takes issue. It's one of those "make your choice" areas. It may initiate complaints but it is also necessary to periodically update or the center will fall into disrepair. This would lead to a poor appearance which will impact how people visualize the quality of your center.

Maintaining the Outdoor Space

The outdoor space includes a great deal of maintenance as well. This space needs regular maintenance in the areas of ensuring the grass is mowed; the area is free of insects which can bite or sting; and the area is free from stray animals. The outdoor space will also need periodic maintenance checks to makes sure that the fence is secure; the yard is free from plants which cause allergic reactions (such as poison ivy); and the gates are working properly. Also take care when evaluating the condition of outdoor toys.

❖ Lesson From the Field: Ongoing Playground maintenance

Alyssa was under the heavy plastic slide toy (not commercial grade) where she was not supposed to be. Kelly (a very large child) was on top jumping up and down as hard as she could. The platform collapsed and fell onto Alyssa's head. There wasn't an injury! I checked multiple times throughout the day to insure she was ok. An incident report was completed to inform the parent and the toy was removed from the playground.

Children can be rough on toys and when the toys are damaged and fall into disrepair, they may present hazards to the children. Any toy which is not in good and safe working condition must be moved out of the enclosed playground area for repair or discarding. The "use zone" or filled outdoor area must be evaluated periodically. This is the area which is padded with some sort of material to cushion a fall and help children have a safer landing. It is generally required to surround higher climbing toys, swings, or other outdoor toys as specified in your licensing standards. The fill can be made up of materials such as pea gravel, shredded rubber playground fill, sand, or other such material. It will pack down over time and much of it also winds up outside the use zone. The fill material needs to be evaluated and replaced as needed to maintain the depth required by the licensing standards.

Handling Emergencies and Disruptions

There are times when even the best prepared and maintained center will face challenges. Events that create challenges are complicated by the fact that the director not only has to take care of the actual problem, but there are many small children who are impacted and must be cared for appropriately even during difficult situations. Severe weather and power outages fall within this category. When the power goes out it is not only dark for children but electric ovens used to prepare food don't work. It can also become very hot or very cold inside the building depending on the time of year. Think about how these types of events should be handled, prepare your staff, and be ready so that these bad situations are not made worse due to a lack of preparation.

Emergency drills need to be practiced regularly so that the staff and children know what to do in an emergency. Fire drills are the most prevalent but there are others such as severe weather drills. Emergency procedures should be established and drills practiced. Make sure your staff knows how they will direct the children so that they are best protected in severe weather such as tornados. Also, be prepared for volumes of phone calls during the middle of such storms as many parents are trying to call and check on the safety of their children. Positive reassurance will help the parents deal with the scare of the event as well.

The emergency procedures should include a plan in the rare case that the building should have to be evacuated. An example requiring evacuation would be a gas leak. Where will you take the children? How will you transport them?

Temporary Closures

Extreme conditions which can impact the center include severe storms and power outages. Another potential for shut down would be voluntary based on bad road conditions, ice, storms, hurricanes, etc. Emergency weather procedures should be in place and the staff should be aware of how to proceed in such conditions.

If conditions continue for hours and impact your center's operation, it may be necessary to call the parents. If needed, you can decide to close the center and call the parent to come pick up their children. Be aware that someone (and it should be the manager) will need to be there for a long time as you wait for every last child to be picked up.

Just as there are conditions which require you to close on a rare occasion, there are also conditions which will mean that you can't open. These usually take the form of major events such as extreme snow, ice, hurricanes, or other somewhat predictable circumstances. If you can foresee that there may be a need to close, let the parents know ahead of time.

Policies for closing should be a part of your parent handbook. It should state under what conditions you will close and how you will determine whether or not to close. One good way is to follow the local school district. Your closing policy can say that you follow the school district's closings. If they close the local schools, then you will close as well. This way parents can listen to the local news and know whether or not you will be open. This is also a way to stay connected if you keep school-age children. If the schools are open and you are closed then someone still may have to go and get the school-age children from school. It makes a nice coordination of local services and ease of information when you follow the school district's policy. There are also times when you may find yourself anxiously waiting their decision, since you aren't sure whether you will be open or not.

If you are anticipating severe weather, or even just think "maybe" it will be that bad, go ahead and put a note on the door reminding parents of your policy for closure and how they can find out if you will be closed. It may be written in your policies but people forget or they may not have actually read all the policies in the first place. You have to help them avoid negative surprises such as showing up on a bad weather day when the center is closed.

❖ Lesson From the Field: Hurricane Ike

Hurricane Ike made its way along the Texas Gulf Coast in September 2008. We knew it was headed our way days ahead of time. We watched the weather reports hoping that it would turn and head another direction but it didn't seem to be changing its course. We followed the school district's closures because it made sense when our schedules and children were directly tied to the local schools (including taking children to and from school every day). It looked almost certain that they would need to close the school; therefore, we would follow and close our center. The district officials waited until late that evening to make the call. In addition, along the same time, we were contacted by the local fire marshal who told us we would be required to close as well. This was a safety issue as mandatory evacuations were being called for the entire area including our city.

We had put a note on the door that said if the school district closed that we would as well ... just a reminder of our policies. Since it was after closing, I then chose to head back to the center and call every home to advise them that we would be closed until further notice. I made all of the contacts before proceeding home to make arrangements for my own family's evacuation of the area.

Hurricane Ike hit the gulf coast. We waited for it to pass and then headed back as soon as it cleared. All of the power was out throughout the towns as we headed back into the area. It was a long trip with great delays as all of the traffic lights, in town after town, were now four way stops. After many hours, we made it back into our town and were lucky to find only a great deal of clean up without substantial damage. After many hours of cleaning up branches, trees, and trash from the storm, we waited to have the power restored. I put notes on the front door, knowing that families would be checking to see when we would re-open. We couldn't open back up until we had power ... we waited two weeks to get our power back. It was our longest closure.

Don't forget when making those policies to include how you will handle tuition on days when the center is closed. If you will not be refunding tuition for the emergency closure, be sure to include that in your policies. This is acceptable in most circumstances and will rarely be a point of issue with parents for a single day closure due to weather. When you have extended closures which go on for days or even weeks, such as the event of a hurricane, then it may be necessary to make other arrangements. The parents may be paying for alternative childcare, be out of work for some time, and have additional burdens placed on them.

It is rare, but there are instances when the school can be closed by a regulatory agency. The most obvious one would be state licensing. In this circumstance the center would usually have had warning if it were due to ongoing violations of state childcare licensing standards. This type of closure could also happen without prior notice if a significant event occurred, such as an injury or death of a child due to neglect or lack of supervision. This is also why the state inspector will visit more often, if you do not demonstrate that your center is operating safely and according to licensing standards. There are centers with numerous violations which continue to operate; however, licensing standards which impact the health, safety, and security of children in care are the ones that are more likely to lead to a closure by the state childcare agency.

Another uncommon but potential source of shutting down is the health department. This can happen in instances where there are excessive cases of illness within the center. This is particularly true when those cases are required to be reported to the health agency or there is an outbreak in the local area and it is well known. The health department has the ability to close the business temporarily to stop the spread of illness throughout the center. This falls under the same concept as when public schools are closed due to rampant outbreaks of an illness. The close confines of schools and childcare centers can make the spread of illness a very difficult challenge at times.

21

Curriculum and Environment

In this chapter, you will learn the importance of curriculum and environment in your program including:

- Overview of Curriculum and Environment
- School Culture and Environment
- Creating a Niche
- Curriculum
- Materials
- Process Over Product
- Parties, Celebrations, and Birthdays
- Animals in Childcare

Overview of Curriculum and Environment

Quality early childhood programs with positive environments and well designed curriculum can provide a wonderful foundation for children's growth and learning. Good programs should take many elements into consideration. These programs should maintain a focus on research and creativity to produce ideal programs for enhancing early childhood education.

School Culture and Environment

The culture and environment of the childcare center is absolutely critical and should be directly tied to the mission of the center. What is it that you are trying to accomplish? What is the foundational philosophy of the center? What niche are you working to fill? The culture and environment are the essence of what the center is all about. This is the atmosphere of the school. These elements make up the essence of what is felt as parents and children walk into the school.

Is it a relaxed and busy play based environment? Is it a stricter school like environment? Whatever the philosophy of the school and the need it is designed to fill, the environment should correctly reflect this.

Environment can be made up of many elements. These elements include the atmosphere as it is felt; whether or not background music is used; and what curriculum if any is used. The entire feel of the center should be based on the mission that it is designed to create. Remember, childcare is much more than just a business. It should be a mission with a real desire to make a difference in the lives of children. The environment of the center should actively reflect this mission.

Good communication policies are an essential part of a positive culture and a successful center. Parents need communication that is effective, useful, and timely. Posting notes on the doors can be an effective way of keeping parents up to date on schedules and events. Sending notes home is important if the message is personal such as discipline or reminders to bring more diapers. By writing the information down, the parent has a written reminder. This can be much more effective than telling them or putting a note on the door. An individual note is less likely to be forgotten, as it can actually go home with the parent and be kept. Sending notes home is also a good idea if your dates and events list is long and has many details. This can be particularly important at holiday times when there are a number of different events going on. It is also important when there are more details to remember such as the date; time of the party; something to bring for the party; and a gift to share at the party.

Suggestions for positive communication include:

- ✓ Make it happy: Use cute preschool graphics or purchased cute appropriate paper for notes and reminders
- ✓ Post door notes: Remind parents of events, parties, and tuition due dates
- ✓ Parent notes: Put it in writing ... bring diapers, behavior notes, and other reminders

Even with all you do to send communication home and prepare parents for events, there will be times when parents forget important details. They are busy and depend on your center for support. Be ready to provide for those forgetful moments. It will ease parents' minds and they will be grateful for your help and support. Important ways to do this include having extra sets of clothes in case on potty accidents or spills. These can be easily obtained from your own home or ask parents to bring a few sets of outgrown clothes to donate to the center. Keep a stash of extra diapers, wipes, and training pants for those children who run out and their parents forgot to bring more.

Parties include special considerations. Prepare for the parents who forget to bring something to the party. This could be the cookies that you asked them to bring or the gift for a gift exchange. Have enough extra of all the needed items to cover such events. I am aware of many centers that use the policy that if a child's parent forgets to bring a gift for the Christmas gift exchange (or other such events), the child is left out. This is an absolutely unbelievable and heartbreaking practice in my opinion! The child is devastated to be left out of a very important children's event. It is a simple solution and a good practice to purchase some inexpensive extra gifts to quickly sneak into the party if needed. We often went through a number of such gifts at a single party. None of the children in my center ever went home feeling sad or left out because a parent forgot to pick up something for a party.

Creating a Niche

Creating a marketable niche is a clear component of a center that stands out. Who do you serve? What ages of children? What curriculum do you offer? What is your teaching methodology? What activities do you provide?

❖ Lesson From the Field: A Niche Market

I established a center to provide a Montessori-based education preschool with extended childcare along with after school programs which included academic assistance in a structured environment. At the time there were not any Montessori programs in the area. This also meant that I had to educate people on what "Montessori" was and the benefits it provided to children. It took a little while to build a reputation being based on something very different and more expensive than traditional programs with a play base.

I strived to implement quality at every turn. The center was established to be clean, well managed, and provide a positive learning environment. I designed my own custom curriculum. Much in this industry is done by word of mouth. My center earned a strong reputation of a quality early childhood center, where children routinely performed well above grade level.

As you work and establish something different, don't be surprised when others attempt to use your words in their advertisements and copy your programs. It is the concept of "imitation is the best flattery" in practice. If it happens, it means you are doing something that others are truly taking notice of. How do you respond? Continue to work on constantly improving and providing the best possible program based on your own goals and ideals. Stay true to your focus and continually get better. If others sound like you in their ads … change your ads. Be the leader and stay a step ahead.

When you create a high quality program, parents will pay more. It is a good thing and it is necessary to support the costs of running a high end program. Be aware also that parents' expectations are higher and they will often readily let you know when they are not happy. Many of those issues from a child with a boo-boo to a problem with your menu will begin with "I pay a lot of money …" They do and they deserve the quality program promised; however, some will have expectations that can't be correctly resolved or aligned to what you know is best for your center and your children as a whole. Fix what you can as it aligns with your policies and staying true to your mission. If you can't fix it or it's not right to do so, let them know. Then have those parents make their own decisions as to whether your program remains right for them.

Curriculum

Curriculum is at the heart of a quality early childhood program. Curriculum programs can be play-based or academic-based. Even within these categories, there are many options. Play-based can be about mostly free play, themed play units, and even filled with projects and art. Academic-based programs vary widely as well. These programs can be based on fundamental basic academics, purchased curriculum, Montessori curriculum, all the way to high level advanced academic programs which include accomplishing reading and math at grade levels well above pre-kindergarten. Determine what it is that your center is designed to accomplish and make sure that the curriculum chosen is appropriate for your mission.

Typical curriculum elements include certain components. These components are an important part of most quality early childhood centers. These include basic art materials, projects, books, toys, and activities. Quality curriculum should take into account the different learning styles of children and incorporate multiple learning styles within the lessons and activities so that all children benefit fully.

Materials

Inexpensive art supplies can be an important part of a good program. Art is important for many reasons for young children. It provides creativity, exploration, a sense of accomplishment, and much more. The benefits are huge. It's an area that should be readily embraced and utilized often in early childhood education. Art projects can be purchased, but much of the best art is basic and inexpensive. Giving children some basic art supplies and a few creative suggestions can lead them on their way to creating their own master pieces. Good art materials not only allow for creativity but help children with fine motor skills as well.

Basic art materials include paper, crayons, pencils, and scissors. Other material ideas include foam shapes, stickers, play dough, sculpting clay, glitter, and other items. Be careful to monitor the use of scissors. It's almost inevitable that in time someone will either cut their own hair at school, or worse, cut someone else's hair. Painting with brushes and finger paint can also make fun art projects. There are many other inexpensive items which can be added to the art supplies. These provide extra creative insights. For the best results, alternate which materials are used rather than setting them all out on a regular basis. Items which are rotated are more interesting since it feels like there are new materials more often.

It is a wonderful feeling of accomplishment for children, to make art that they are proud of to take home and show their parents. This should be done often as a regular part of all childcare programs. It also provides parents with additional insight into what their children were able to learn and do during the day.

Process Over Product

The most important part of art in early childhood is for both the teachers and parents to recognize the concept of process over product. Early childhood art is about learning, exploration, and having fun ... not about the end result. Make sure that your staff understands the value of this. Teachers shouldn't "fix" projects to make them better. They should appreciate what the child was able to accomplish. Explain or better yet, have the children explain their "masterpiece creations" to their parents. No, it's not a mess of food thrown together; it is a creative cooking project with real learning objectives!

Parties, Celebrations, and Birthdays

Parties are a lot of fun and if they fit into your program's philosophy they should be included. Determine which holidays you will celebrate. Also determine what celebrating a birthday at your center will include. Specify what is allowed and provide that information to parents in your policies.

As you do this keep in mind that even if your center's beliefs and policies include parties, not all of your families may believe or feel the same way. Know your families, their beliefs and needs and how you will accommodate these when they differ from yours.

❖ Lesson From the Field: Holidays and Varying Beliefs

My center was a Christian based center. We included the celebration of birthdays and holidays, including Christmas and Easter. At the same time we had a few families who had different beliefs. These beliefs included Muslim and Jehovah's Witness. It was necessary to make appropriate adjustments for these children.

We made our philosophies clear when parents visited us and chose to enroll. They knew what we believed and what we celebrated and this enabled them to make their choices accordingly. In addition, we made adjustments to the degree it was possible for families who chose to join us but whose beliefs were different from the majority of our families.

Animals in Childcare

Some programs will include animals as a means of interest, learning, and science lessons for young children. A number of considerations need to be carefully analyzed prior to adding animals into your childcare center. Begin with the state regulations. Most will have specific rules regarding what animals may be included in the program and which animals may not be included. Some of the options may even be quite surprising. An example would be Texas regulations, do not allow numerous types of animals which are commonly used in education programs. " ... Children must not have contact with chickens, ducks, and reptiles, such as snakes, turtles, lizards, iguanas, and amphibians, such as frogs and toads." Minimum Standards for Child-Care Centers, Texas Department of Family and Regulatory Services, 2010, Page 130-A.

Make sure that as you design your curriculum and programs so that each step is feasible within the confines of state regulations. There are times when it feels like regulations and safety are confining and eliminate what could be very good educational curriculum projects such as watching baby chicks hatch or seeing the transformation from tadpole to frog. The reality is that it isn't a choice that center administrators should make. Licensed facilities must work within the confines of state regulations and adhere to those requirements, even when it means giving up some great hands-on learning opportunities for children.

Some of the best animals for a childcare center are fish and very small rodents such as hamsters, mice, and gerbils. These small animals fit within the scope of most state regulations. Because they live in contained habitats, children are able to enjoy them, observe them, and learn without endangering the child or animal. Always be careful when handling small animals such as hamsters. It can be a wonderful opportunity to "pet" the hamster but it must be of a calm disposition; held by the teacher; and petting should be carefully explained as "one finger" gently petting the top of the animal. Regular procedures must also include hand washing of all children after gently petting the animal.

❖ Lesson From the Field: Hamsters Escape

Their nocturnal escapades seem to include living for the opportunity to find a way out of the cage. This includes pulling up on water bottles, spending hours piling all of the bedding in one area to reach the top of the cage etc. I have to admit, I had a couple of escape artist hamsters over the years. The good news is they weren't hard to catch as I could catch them in a small live animal trap at night when they returned to the cage area for food.

Keep in mind that if you choose to have animals, even very small animals, they do add quite a bit of work to the programs. This includes trips back to feed and check on them on weekends and cleaning cages. Choose your housing for small pets carefully. Keep in mind that smaller animals such as the tiniest hamsters can escape through wire cages meant for regular sized hamsters. Cages must be cleaned regularly both for sanitation and for odor control. Clear plastic cages for small animals with mesh sliding tops tend to control odor better and protect small animals inside a center.

Fish make great pets in childcare centers. These require minimal effort and weekend feedings include throwing in a weekend feeder tablet. One last detail in mind with small pets is: How will you handle or explain the death of a pet? Be ready to explain … or if you choose quickly replace in the case of death.

22

Sustaining Long Term Success

In this chapter, you will learn the secrets to sustained success through ongoing enrollment and marketing including:

- Sustaining Long Term Success Overview
- Phone Inquiries
- Information Packets
- Prospective Parent Visits
- Unscheduled Visits
- Continuing to Share with Parents

Sustaining Long Term Success Overview

Sustaining success means a real focus on quality programs, safety, exceptional curriculum, and excellent staff, along with a real effort placed toward ongoing enrollment and marketing. Great programs and people will build your center's reputation and enrollment. The best marketing that a center can have is word of mouth. Successful childcare businesses are based in great programs which lead to happy parents. Happy parents tell their friends and the word spreads. This is the foundation of ongoing success.

Phone Inquiries

As the word spreads and more new parents call with inquiries into your center. These calls become more frequent and can be time consuming, but they are absolutely vital to ongoing success. Make sure that the director or someone else in charge takes the time to do more than quote a price for childcare. Phone calls often begin with the question: "How much do you charge for a two year old?" … or other ages as appropriate.

Most centers have someone pick up the phone and simply answer the few questions that are asked:

- ✓ "Do you have room for a three year old?"
- ✓ "How much do you charge?"
- ✓ "What time do you close?"

First note that childcare centers, even those with well designed programs, can be noisy at times and that noise can be very distracting to a caller asking questions. Even if it is a busy classroom of happy working preschoolers, it can sound like chaos on the other end of the line. If possible, step into the office or a quiet classroom so that you can focus on the phone call in a professional manner and eliminate the distracting background noise as you answer questions for the caller. If it is not possible to do this, then it is best to make a quick apology; explain that you are working with children inside a classroom right now; and ask if you can take the caller's name and phone number. Get back to her when you are able to spend dedicated time with her and fully answer all of her questions.

If your center is offering a quality program, then the director should have a great deal more information to share with people than simply answering those basic questions. This is a time to look away from that pile of papers that is stacked on the desk and really talk about what your program offers children. What are the benefits? What makes you different? Talk about that niche that your program fills, your mission, and what you can do for the caller's child.

First, let's address the answer to the first and most popular inquiry: "How much do you charge?" A good answer is not the cost printed on the tuition sheet. Instead answer with "Are you familiar with our programs?" If the caller is not, then tell her about the fantastic programs; what the children learn; how great the staff is; and everything else that parent should learn about your program to help her make a good decision regarding whether it is right for her child. It is best to spend time explaining the programs and not reveal the tuition until later. Centers which provide high quality programs will cost more. It is a good strategy to sell the parents on the quality of the program first.

On occasion this will result in a frustrated parent who really did just want to know if you were the cheapest center in town. It is truly amazing at times that some parents really do shop for childcare like they shop for toilet paper … just looking for what is the cheapest. If you are managing a quality center with great programs and staff, it is unlikely that you are going to be the place for this parent. It's okay; this wasn't the right program for that parent.

More often, you will find a parent on the other end who is truly interested in what your program has to offer. Often the parent doesn't know what to ask other than the basics such as cost and hours. It's your opportunity to fill in what he should know about the center. Provide the information that he didn't know he needed to ask. Often you will get a positive response with a request to schedule a visit to come in and see the center and visit your classes. Those calls are worth the time and effort. These lead to new enrollment which is what you need for sustained success. I often received comments that no one else provided that much information. Hook them on the call with how good the programs are. Save rates for last, after all of the other information.

As you spend significant time talking to parents who inquire about the programs, remember that you never know where that will lead. Even parents who do not sign up their own children will talk to other parents. This can lead to other parents coming in for information and signing up their children. There are times when grandparents come in to learn about programs. Spend just as much time with noncustodial grandparents as with parents. The same can be said for those information packets that should always be available for anyone who asks. You don't know where they will end up. Often they are used by parents, there are other times where these packets are passed on to a friend who has children and is interested in the programs.

Information Packets

Create an information packet which explains your program in detail. Make it attractive with pictures of your facility and children's activities along with information on your programs and tuition rates. (Be sure to get written permission from parents before including children's pictures in your promotional materials.) This is one of the best marketing tools that you will have. The information packet can also contain the enrollment forms if you want. This keeps all the information ready for parents when they visit the center.

Keep the information packets stocked and available. These should be a part of each scheduled parent visit. It provides all of the information that you want parents to know about your programs including hours, rates, curriculum, and policies. Having these available makes it easier for staff members to provide information to parents who arrive unannounced. In situations where a staff member is not able to stop what she is doing and give a full tour to a prospective parent who drops in, this provides valuable information which can be given to the parent. Have the staff member get the name and phone number of the parent so that she can be contacted later to schedule a visit.

There are even times, when this is really all a parent wants. They drop in while they are out running errands and don't have time to come in and receive a full informational tour of the center. Providing a packet puts all the pertinent information in their hands. It provides all the valuable things that your center does along with the rate sheet and enrollment forms.

Prospective Parent Visits

Scheduled and unscheduled visits are another important form of ongoing enrollment. Scheduled visits are often made during the initial phone call. Ironically, it is fairly typical for parents to not show up for a scheduled appointment. People change their minds, or their circumstances change and many do not feel the need to cancel the appointment; they just don't show up. Don't let this deter you. Continue to spend time on the phone; share your program with everyone who calls and wants to listen; and continue to make appointments for parents to visit the center.

Parent visits to the center are a huge opportunity to show off your programs. If your programs are really good, it will show. Parents will be able to see the difference. The best times to schedule appointments are during your lesson times, if your center provides lessons. This is where you will be able to show the parents the benefits of the program and how their children's lessons will take place. Take time to let parents see inside the classrooms; explain how the program works; and discuss the benefits that the program provides. Seeing is believing. This is where your programs will shine.

If the visitors have time, go ahead and take them through all the rooms. This shows them the entire center and how the quality continues throughout all of the classrooms. This is even more important if their children are very young and will potentially be enrolled in your programs over a period of years. This also provides information that parents will often share with their friends and may lead to more inquiries and more students.

Just as with phone interviews, provide all of the benefits and program information first and tuition last. This is the time to really show what you offer. There is a reason that tuition is higher. It is because you offer more. It is fine to directly say that. You have to charge more because of all that is provided in your program.

Quality early childhood programs can really make a difference for children. It can provide a great foundation for behavior, manners, hygiene, fine motor skills, large motor skills, and academic learning. Choosing a quality program is an investment. Be direct and explain how your program can make a difference for the child, based on what you offer and the benefits. Many parents do sacrifice and do without some other things to be able to provide quality programs for their children during their very early years. It can be a very good investment with long term benefits.

❖ Lesson From the Field: Long Term Benefits

I still see parents in town and at school functions with my own children. One of the greatest rewards that I receive is when parents see me and credit their child's early academic success to their time in my early childhood program. That was what my program was designed to do and it's wonderful to see parents who are happy and found that the program was a good investment for their child.

Unscheduled Visits

It is common for people to "pop in" unannounced to visit the center. This is a great opportunity as well. If at all possible, drop whatever you were doing and take the time to show the center at that point in time. This often seems to be at naptime (because parents are on a lunch break from work) which is one of the most difficult times to show how great your program is. Go ahead and explain how things are done during your lesson time and how the day unfolds for the children. Explain the benefits, provide information, and invite the parent to schedule an appointment to visit during a time where you are able to show them more by visiting your classes while the children are busy learning.

Even when centers are at or near capacity, it is important to take the time to do a good job in representing the school. If there aren't openings, you can begin a waiting list. Waiting lists create an opportunity to fill positions when children withdraw. Children can be withdrawn from programs on very short notice and sometimes families just stop coming without any notice at all. A waiting list allows you to fill those places quickly with less impact on finances.

Be aware that a waiting list is not really as valuable as it may appear on paper. A list with ten names may only pan out to be a few children in reality. The reason is that parents are looking for childcare at a certain period in time. Some will wait for a position to come open. In contrast, many will not enroll if you don't have an opening at the time they are ready. Once they enroll somewhere else, they are much less likely to withdraw their child from that center because you have an opening at a later date.

Continuing to Share with Parents

There is a great deal of effort that goes into providing information for parents so that they understand the benefits of your program. Don't forget to continue this sharing and letting parents know what you are doing for their children after they have enrolled. This is a very important component of continued success.

Reinvest in your center. Each year, determine what you can do to continue to provide great quality programs. This includes physical items such as building updates, new furniture, and new toys. It also includes program updates such as reviewing and editing curriculum and adding new academic materials. As you review these things and provide new things, let your parents know. Put a note on the door or send home a little notice that you are excited about the new materials that you are adding to your science program. Send your staff members to conference to get new ideas, learn new songs, and have them bring these things back to your children. Send home a note that says the teachers went to the conference and they are doing these new activities with the children.

Making changes that benefit the families, children, and the environment should be included in this list. If you add new updates, even those required by changing regulations, let parents know that you have done that. Tell the parents how these updates will benefit their children. If you decide to implement a paper recycling program, have the children participate and let the parents know that you are committed to taking care of the environment for the long term benefit of the children's generation.

Create an evaluation system for students. This can be relatively simple all the way up to full standardized testing. One of the easiest to implement is a portfolio system. Have teachers save samples of work throughout the year which represent the child's ability and progress. Even when parents know their children are learning, it is amazing to see real comparisons of work that show what the children learned. An example would be: including samples of how the children wrote letters in August, and including samples of how they wrote those same letters in May.

Other forms of evaluation can include reading skills, fine motor skills, vocabulary skills, social skills, and much more. Again, what is assessed should be determined based on the mission of the center. The focus of your program should provide information on what and how to evaluate the children's progress. Providing a form of evaluation lets parents really appreciate how much their child has done and learned in a school year. Other good communication strategies include meetings where you can share information about the child's progress as well as address any concerns parents may have.

- ❖ Lesson From the Field: Making Re-Enrollment Positive

    Each year in April, I would have meetings with parents to complete registration for the summer and next school year. At these meetings, I would bring a full evaluation packet that we had completed for each child. As the parents sat down and waited for the meeting, they were able to look through all of the paperwork which demonstrated what their child learned in the current school year. This provided a wonderful opportunity for parents to see their child's progress and it was very motivating as parents were enrolling for the next year. It had additional benefits as happy parents met together and discussed their children's progress. Some parents who were newer to the program were able to find additional benefits as parents who had been with the program for years shared success stories. Often these stories were of their older children who had already completed the preschool program and were having great success and often had advanced placement in their public school classes.

    At these meetings parents were positive as they received information on how much their child had learned in the year, the exciting summer schedule that we had planned, and the plans for the following school year. These meetings also included the supply fees and tuition rates for the following school year. It was a positive way to provide for registering for the following school year.

- ❖ Lesson From the Field: Keeping the Momentum Going

    Our final event each school year was a wonderful "Graduation and Celebration" for all of our children not just pre-kindergarten and kindergarten graduates. It was a great deal of work but it was also our star performance of the year. Happy parents, grandparents, and family members spent a fun afternoon together. Each class of children danced, sang, and received awards for all of their hard work during the school year. It was a phenomenal way to end a school year and there is nothing better than having lots of happy parents join together to talk about the school and their children's progress.

Keep the parents invested and excited about what their children are learning and the environment that they are working in. As you continue to do great things for the children in your care, make sure you share all that you are doing with the parents. Throughout the process, working with parents and children, communication is the big key to major success in childcare. It is a business of heart. It requires a focus on caring with a concern for the day to day, along with a goal of providing long term benefits for the children. There are few fields which make such a huge difference in the lives of children and families than high quality programs which are truly dedicated to meeting the needs of families. Success comes from long hours, hard work and dedication.

Quality childcare is an ongoing process and providing a quality environment counts. As years pass by the reputation grows ever stronger as parents share happy stories of the benefits your program provides with other family members and friends. This provides your ability to sustain, grow, and thrive for years to come.

Andrea Hendon Busch, Ed.D. is an educational specialist with a doctorate degree in Educational Administration and Supervision. She is a certified public school teacher, certified public school administrator, and a state licensed childcare director. Dr. Busch has been an educator for 20 years. She is an experienced classroom teacher, early childhood administrator, and curriculum designer. Dr. Busch has studied extensively in the field of early childhood education. She has researched programs and philosophies in the United States as well as international programs including travel to China to visit preschools and consulting with educators in China.

Dr. Busch designed, founded, managed, and directed a successful childcare center in the state of Texas for nine years. She currently provides professional information including childcare consulting services and on-site training for centers in Texas. Dr. Busch can be contacted at andreab@windsonghollowranch.com for additional information on speaking, training, and consulting programs.

www.ingramcontent.com/pod-product-compliance
Lightning Source LLC
Chambersburg PA
CBHW080543170426
43195CB00016B/2655